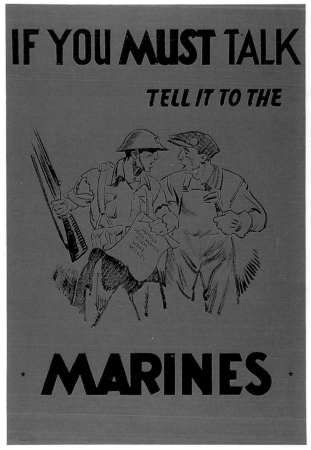

now part of the Political History Collection of the Division of Social History. One strength of the collection is that it contains posters from a wide sampling of government agencies, businesses, and charitable organizations. Another important feature of the collection is that several industrial corporations responded to Tolman's solicitation letter by contributing complete series of the posters appearing in their factories. Viewing these series reveals a promotional strategy that is lost when viewing only a single poster.

To fully understand and appreciate the direct and indirect messages of these posters, it is necessary to place them in their historical context and to consider the motivations of those who commissioned, designed, and posted them. We have chosen to examine the expectations and intent of poster producers at the outset of the war, the debate on how best to communicate war aims through the poster medium, the place of these posters in wartime production, and the aims and values expressed through their imagery.

ABOVE LEFT | *Curator R. P. Tolman in the United States National Museum*

ABOVE RIGHT | *An example of print technique that Tolman acquired in 1942 from the Smithsonian Institution War Committee*

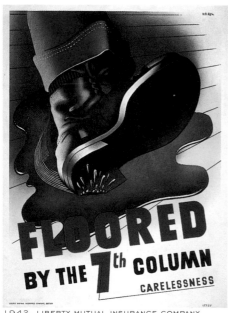

1942. LIBERTY MUTUAL INSURANCE COMPANY

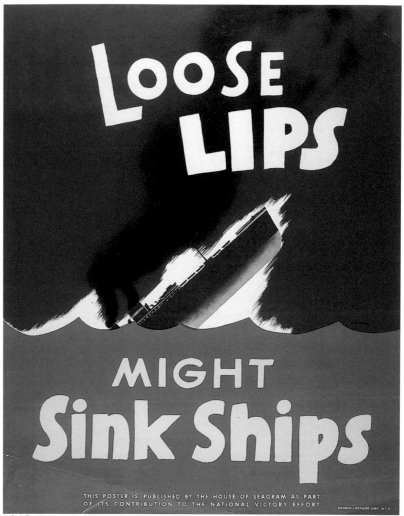

1942. SEAGRAM DISTILLERS CORPORATION

1942. RCA MANUFACTURING COMPANY

1942. GENERAL ELECTRIC COMPANY

"*Thanks a million!*"

TO BOEING WORKER
10 and 100
WAR BOND BUYERS

YOU HAVE WON THE BULLS EYE AND MINUTE MAN FLAGS!

"Congratulations on fine results.
Your record is a splendid accomplishment.
You have the honor of being the first in the
aircraft industry to reach this goal.
Your achievement will encourage others."
Henry Morgenthau, Jr.,
Secretary of the Treasury.

1942. BOEING AIRCRAFT COMPANY

GIVE
WAR
BONDS

The Present with a FUTURE

1943. U.S. TREASURY DEPARTMENT

"**Even a little
can help a lot - *NOW***"

Buy
U.S. WAR STAMPS ★ BONDS

ILLUSTRATION COURTESY OF LADIES' HOME JOURNAL

U.S.GOVERNMENT PRINTING OFFICE : 1942—O—455803 FORM 0SS-405

1942. U.S. TREASURY DEPARTMENT

ATTACK ATTACK ATTACK

BUY WAR BONDS

1942. UNATTRIBUTED

YOU MUST HELP!

RETAILERS FOR VICTORY
We Are Cooperating

BUY WAR STAMPS
This Store's Best Buy

1942. HARRIS, SEYBOLD, POTTER COMPANY

AMERICA CALLING

Take your place in
CIVILIAN DEFENSE

CONSULT YOUR NEAREST DEFENSE COUNCIL

1941. OFFICE OF CIVILIAN DEFENSE

YOU CAN ASSIST
YOUR COUNTRY
YOUR
EMPLOYER and YOURSELF

BY
SAVING
OF ALL
MATERIALS
USED IN THE LITHOGRAPHIC
INDUSTRY
AND AVOIDING
WASTE and ERRORS

PAPER · INKS · CHEMICALS
PLATES
MACHINES and ALL SUPPLIES
ARE SCARCE
DURING THE EMERGENCY
AMALGAMATED
LITHOGRAPHERS
OF AMERICA

1942. AMALGAMATED LITHOGRAPHERS
OF AMERICA

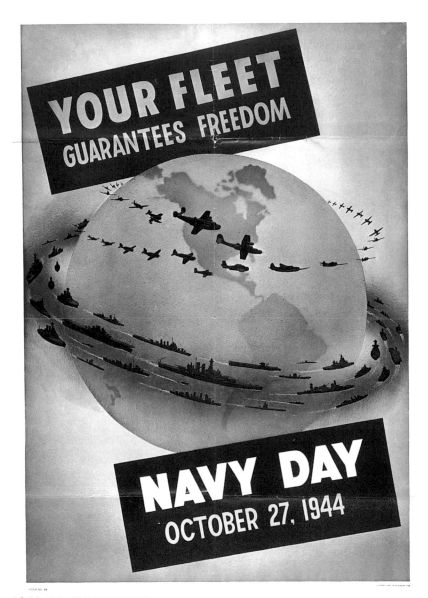

1944. U.S. NAVY DEPARTMENT

WE CAN . . .
WE WILL . .
WE MUST !
..Franklin D. Roosevelt

BUY U.S. WAR SAVINGS BONDS & STAMPS *NOW*

1942. U.S. TREASURY DEPARTMENT

ABOVE | *This image, said to be the most popular poster design of World War II, appeared as a billboard in 1941. Carl Paulson created the design under the direction of the Outdoor Advertising Association of America, Inc., for a U.S. Treasury Department campaign promoting the widespread public ownership of defense bonds and stamps. To demonstrate the power of advertising while selling bonds, the billboard industry displayed this image of the American flag at more than 30,000 locations in some 18,000 cities and towns across the country in March and April 1942. The Treasury brought back the billboard for campaigns in July 1942 and 1943. To meet public demand for copies of the billboard, the Government Printing Office also printed four million small color reproductions.[2]*

1942. PONTIAC MOTOR DIVISION, GENERAL MOTORS CORPORATION

CHAPTER ONE

THE POSTER'S PLACE IN WARTIME

I n 1940, the poster was one of several media in a landscape of commercial promotion that had hardly existed twenty years before. An increasingly mobile audience shaped by commercial radio, motion pictures, magazines, and billboards populated this environment. Posters, in fact, were usually seen in the form of 24-sheet billboards. By contrast, the single-sheet posters deployed in World War II were small. Seeking the "place of the poster" in late 1942, critic Alfred M. Frankenfurter noted that though small posters "did not play a major part in publicity," this fact lent them "the advantage of freshness along with the awkwardness of novelty."[3] With the coming of the Second World War, champions of the poster's resurgence saw in postings a direct reflection of the spirit of a community. As one U.S. Office of War Information (OWI) official put it, "We want to see posters on fences, on the walls of buildings, on village greens, on boards in front of the City Hall and the Post Office, in hotel lobbies, in the windows of vacant stores—not limited to the present neat conventional frames which make them look like advertising, but shouting at people from unexpected places with all the urgency which this war demands."[4] "Ideally," another confirmed, "it should be possible to post America every night. People should wake up to find a visual message everywhere, like new snow—every man, woman and child should be reached and moved by the message."[5] Aspiring to become the official clearinghouse for government poster design and distribution, OWI's dollar-a-year men, drawn from the ranks of advertising, established overlapping systems of distribution modeled

LEFT | *Posters pasted to a corrugated building on the working ways at the Pennsylvania shipyards, May 1943*

RIGHT | *Exhibit of government posters in the U.S. Information Service in the Temporary V building at 14th Street and Pennsylvania Avenue, Washington, D.C., June 1942*

upon the elaborate volunteer organization set up during the First World War.[6] A national network placed posters in such venues as post offices, railroad stations, schools, restaurants, and retail-store groups. At the local level, OWI arranged distribution through volunteer defense councils, whose members selected appropriate posting places, established posting routes, ordered posters from supply catalogs, and took the "Poster Pledge." The "Poster Pledge" urged volunteers to "avoid waste," treat posters "as real war ammunition," "never let a poster lie idle," and "make every one count to the fullest extent."[7]

Across Washington, officials of the U.S. Office for Emergency Management's War Production Board (WPB)

specialized in production-incentive images for factories. Under the direction of Vaughn Flannery, William B. Phillips, and Charles T. Coiner, the WPB led the way in contracting with commercial illustrators and designers for posters.[8] The WPB's Poster Catalog (1942) offered a selection of twenty-three single-sheet posters and placards ranging in size from 7-by-10 to 56-by-40 inches. The WPB also offered three 16 ¾-inch-by-10-foot "streamers," "for semipermanent displays in relatively difficult posting locations." These featured the slogans, "Time is Short," "United We Stand," and "Every Minute Counts." Distributing posters and streamers free for the asking, the WPB asked in return only that recipients "Select your posting spots with care, and stick to these posting spots....[U]se your imagination in displaying posters and in building up exhibits composed of two, three, or a dozen different kinds of posters." The WPB's posting tips urged factory managers to order enough posters, cautioning that "posters put up in a ration of less than one for each 100 workmen on the shift are usually too thinly spread to be wholly effective."

1942. U.S. OFFICE OF WAR INFORMATION

1942. U.S. WAR PRODUCTION BOARD

LEFT | *OWI officials felt that the most urgent problem on the home front was the careless leaking of sensitive information that could be picked up by spies and saboteurs.*

The WPB's posting guidelines achieved wide circulation in *Business Week* magazine, though its embellishment of the story undercut the agency's confidence in the poster's inherent attention-arresting qualities. *Business Week*'s reportage of the WPB's posting tips included advice never given by the WPB: "Motion is a decided asset. Posters on doors that are fre-quently opened and closed on delivery trucks, giant cranes and other machinery, are endowed with life that still posters do not have."[9] The poster's proponents, however, turned the liabilities of a static medium into advantages. For example, a WPB progress report describing the poster's place at the scene of production exclaimed, "Posters work a *24-hour* shift!"[10]

TOP | *Labor-management cooperation rally making use of a War Production Board streamer, ca. 1942*

BOTTOM | *Workers sealing barrage balloon seams beneath a War Production Board streamer*

FACING PAGE | *Describing the vast number and kind of production incentive posters, Allegheny Ludlum Steel Corporation's company magazine* Steel Horizons *exclaimed, "We've never seen anything like it."*

WORKER MORALE

Going Up!

THESE and the following two pages present a slice of contemporary Americana—a very small sample from the total morale-building effort that is under way.

The first World War brought out a few notable examples of inspirational posters in its Liberty Loans, Red Cross, and recruiting drives; but what was a trickle then, is a flood today. We've never seen anything like it.

It does not originate, this flood of patriotic appeal, in a supposition that the people's morale is lower than in 1917, and therefore needs more whipping up. Rather, it is a reflection of the totality of this war; the fact that it reaches deeper into everyone's life, making greater demands and promising more terrible penalties for failure, than any other war in history. Such a war can only be fought by extraordinary measures, and they must start on the home industrial front.

A man's will to give of himself is directly attuned to his state of mind. That holds for all his relationships—his family, his outside interests, and his job. As morale rises, so does production; and on a front that runs from coast to coast, American industries and war agencies have launched a tremendous drive to lift and sustain the morale of the people. *All* the people, every last member of each family, because this is a people's war.

Individual companies caught fire early. RCA asked its employees to "*Beat the Promise*" and they're doing it. General Electric is "*Beating Time*"; Packard has just launched a "*Work to Win*" campaign. Hundreds of other companies are riding the crest of similar enthusiasms; hundreds more are planning them. The big push is definitely on.

War reporting frequently balloons a little good news into front-page headlines, while burying a lot of bad news on the back pages. Not so with these war-drive posters. They warn and exhort, unify and encourage; but they do not sugar-coat the bitter pill of war. Their language is salty and vigorous, their accent sharp and purposeful; they sound a general note of confidence, but the grim consequence of slackness or failure is harshly implied.

The appeals are various. To pride in America's strength. To preservation of freedom and other American heritages, in jeopardy and worth fighting for. To the importance of each worker's role. To team spirit and the competitive urge, so strongly grained in Americans.

There are many avenues of appeal in a war so fateful, and a year so critical. One expects war agencies to use them. But when private companies—RCA, GE, Packard and all the others—take on the job of inspiration as well as production, you can't shrug it off as dollar patriotism. That, in itself, is good for morale.

★ ★ ★ ★ ★ ★ ★ ★ ★ ★ ★ ★ ★

Almost as familiar to American workers as the face of General MacArthur, whose latest and best portrait comes to you with this issue, are these war posters. Prepared and distributed without charge by the Office for Emergency Management's *Division of Information*, under the capable handling of Robert W. Horton, Director, a continuing series of pertinent and arresting subjects flows out of Washington to war producers, public institutions, etc., all over the country.

3

1942. MAGAZINE SPREAD FROM STEEL HORIZONS, ALLEGHENY LUDLUM STEEL CORPORATION

Recruitment poster in Benton Harbor, Michigan, July 1940

CHAPTER TWO

WAR AIMS THROUGH ART

The poster occupied a special place in the thoughts and plans of wartime artists, illustrators, and a supportive community of museum curators and advertising-agency art directors. The war called forth special skills in the defense of democratic ideals, and museum curators and advertising specialists alike aggressively promoted artists' and illustrators' efforts as war contributions of the first order. As the war progressed, the promotion of expertise in poster design and distribution coexisted uneasily with the democratic rhetoric that embellished the medium's war contribution. Indeed, at the war's outset the poster's made-by-all possibilities and seen-by-all accessibility spoke for a symmetry of democratic technique and effect. For many, this quality made the poster an especially fitting medium for the expression of American war aims: why we fight, what we fight for.[11] The silk-screen shop of New York City's Works Progress Administration (WPA) inspired one the most succinct statements of poster artists' democratic war aims, when an Office of War Information handbook explaining techniques that simplified the serial production of colorful posters declared, "Anyone can make a poster."[12] One of the last remaining New Deal federal arts projects, the New York City WPA won funding from Mayor Fiorello LaGuardia after congressional opposition effectively ended WPA projects elsewhere.[13] From 1941 to 1942 the NYC-WPA's poster output included posters and car cards made to be displayed on city subways, buses, and trains for the American Red Cross and the Department of Agriculture's Rural Electrification Administration.

ALL: 1942, NEW YORK CITY WPA WAR SERVICES

ALL: 1942. NEW YORK CITY WPA WAR SERVICES FOR THE RURAL ELECTRIFICATION ADMINISTRATION,
U.S. DEPARTMENT OF AGRICULTURE

ALL: 1942. NEW YORK CITY WPA WAR SERVICES

Noted for their outwardly democratic design, U.S. Treasury Department savings-bond posters tapped the well-honed skills of commercial illustrators to project a human touch. Treasury officials specifically rejected what historian Jarvis M. Morse describes as the "high pressure" sales techniques associated with the Liberty Loan drives of World War I. In early 1941, Treasury officials began applying the poster to the new goal of securing "widespread ownership of the public debt…'transforming people from being mere observers into becoming active participants…emphasiz[ing] at all times participation rather than propaganda—voluntary cooperation rather than coercion.'" As savings bonds became *defense* bonds, officials redesigned the small-denomination savings stamp to include a new logo featuring Daniel Chester French's "Minuteman at Concord."[14] The Treasury lavished the same attention upon the representation of the working bondholder.

I'm No Millionaire, But… idealized the American bondholder as a ruddy-faced workman in bib overalls. Conceived by illustrators J. Walter Wilkinson and his son Walter G. Wilkinson (who signed their collaborative work "Wilkinsons"), the imagery of work and its patriotic significance anticipated wartime representations of the factory as the front line for decisive action.

The process of making a poster began with a pencil sketch. The Wilkinsons transferred their sketches to canvas using a copying device called a pantograph. The Treasury photographed the painting *You Buy 'em We'll Fly 'em* in final form for mass distribution, in this case an unprecedented print run of 1,500,000 posters. Like *I'm No Millionaire*, the Wilkinsons' *You Buy 'em* featured a human-interest theme to sell bonds and stamps. "[The Wilkinsons] believe," wrote one observer in 1942, "that Americans will respond to the expressions on the faces of men who work in America's factories, who drive tanks into battle and who fly bombers and fighter planes."[15]

BELOW | *Treasury-bond sales booth organized and staffed by the members of the local parent-teacher association, Turlock, California, May 1942*

TOP AND BOTTOM RIGHT: 1941. ORIGINAL ART FOR U.S. TREASURY DEPARTMENT

Working independently and receiving no compensation other than the satisfaction of seeing their work widely reproduced, the Wilkinsons painted five Treasury poster designs, four of which were produced. Treasury officials rejected a fifth painting, of President Franklin D. Roosevelt. J. Walter Wilkinson recalled the officials explaining that picturing FDR at the height of his powers would open their sales campaign to the charge that it was political propaganda.

Despite the *pro bono* contributions of commercial illustrators who established relationships with government officials, the procurement of satisfactory poster designs became a problem in the defense emergency. In April 1941, New York's Museum of Modern Art (MoMA) proposed to enlarge the pool of poster designs with a competition. A press release announced, "The Museum's job is to bring work to the attention of government agencies who need and are commissioning these services." Conversely, the competition would provide artists with an opportunity to demonstrate their "ability and willingness to serve in our national emergency." MoMA officials promoted their competition as an exhibition of trends in contemporary poster design, independent of those continuously displayed on billboards. Artists might enter designs in each of two categories designated for the government's largest users of posters: the Treasury Defense Savings Staff and the U.S. Army Air Corps recruiting effort. MoMA officials took pains to assure potential contestants that neither the advertising-agency art directors nor the government clients advising the museum would unduly influence the contest's outcome. Contributing artists would be "free to express themselves without restraint."[16]

CA. 1942. ORIGINAL ART FOR U.S. TREASURY DEPARTMENT

1941. ORIGINAL ART FOR U.S. TREASURY DEPARTMENT

1941. ORIGINAL ART FOR U.S. TREASURY DEPARTMENT

ABOVE | *Artist John C. Atherton's first prize design for Defense Bonds being posted on a billboard at 42nd Street and 5th Avenue, July 1941.*

1941. U.S. TREASURY DEPARTMENT

1941. OFFICE FOR EMERGENCY MANAGEMENT, DIVISION OF INFORMATION

The winning entry in the defense-bond category, designed by John C. Atherton, confirmed the high-style surrealism of commercial illustration as a trend in poster design. Atherton's commercial work graced the covers of *Fortune* magazine, as well as magazine advertisements conveying "mood" and "feeling" for Sharp & Dohme pharmaceutical products, among others. Describing Atherton as a "part-time Surrealist" and a leading example of an artist engaged in "class advertising," one observer later noted: "What the public wants is a certain juiciness, a plasticity, a sensation of false reality which enables the reader to really see what the thing represented is."[17] The most public manifestation of this trend appeared when Atherton's winning entry in the defense bond category went up on a forty-eight-foot billboard located at one of New York's busiest street corners, 42nd Street and 5th Avenue. The poster featured clasped hands, representing worker and government, superimposed above the smokestacks of a factory.[18]

Government officials judged the MoMA poster competition a mixed success. While Treasury poster consultant Harford Powel enthusiastically snapped up reproduction rights to the winning designs in the bond category, other officials were reluctant to commission designs from artists unaccustomed to poster technique. From the Office for Emergency Management (OEM) came word that "posters require a highly skilled technique which fine artists do not have, and that the whole problem of poster production will be greatly complicated if the government places production on the basis of competition and awards, or something of that sort."[19] As an official of the Office of Facts and Figures (the predecessor agency of the Office of War Information) privately explained, "You just can't let all the painters in the country paint their heads off and make a lot of posters and then slap them up somewhere."[20]

After Japan's attack on Pearl Harbor on December 7, 1941, complaints about government poster design intensified. Overlapping responsibilities and lack of coordination among poster-issuing agencies had left "a hodge-podge of good, mediocre and bad design."[21] The shift of poster themes from "defense" to "victory" rendered existing designs inadequate. "Production for defense," complained one critic, was a "passive theme, not keyed to get action." Others linked the obsolescence of "defense" as a poster theme to the artists and illustrators who had produced them. While the clenched fists of Atherton and OEM favorite Jean Carlu had served well enough as statements of national purpose during the defense emergency, their posters now appeared "slick and ineffectual, commercial but not war art."[22]

Noting the sudden obsolescence of "defense" as a poster theme, critic Manny Farber wrote in the *New Republic* that "Posters are not getting us anywhere by being so indirect they could do for peacetime." Farber disparaged the underlying commercial esthetic of the Treasury's "panty-waist Minute Man number" and the "Cosmopolitan cutey pie school" represented by the illustrators Howard Chandler Christy and James Montgomery Flagg, whose heroes and heroines from the World War I era had become popular again. "Their babes," Farber wrote, "are more lush than ever; so are their men.... All this slush is so beside the point of this desperate war that its morale-building is heading toward the idea that lipstick will win for us."[23]

CHAPTER THREE

ART, ADVERTISING, AND AUDIENCE

When America entered the war the professional interests of art and advertising collided. Artists, commercial illustrators, and mass-media specialists flocked to the government's war effort. Each group held a conception of an audience that could be persuaded, cajoled, or told what needed to be done. Linking techniques of audience engagement with professional aspirations, each sought to validate its own working method as an effective war contribution. Focusing upon government poster design, advertising specialists preached the avoidance of stylized symbols and abstract images, and the use of survey research to establish effective designs. Others argued for sophisticated, more painterly "war graphics" as the effective basis of government poster design. For a time the two approaches coexisted.

In January 1942, the advertising industry offered its services to the government. The newly organized War Advertising Council, made up of leading Madison Avenue advertising agencies, national advertisers, and mass-media outlets, placed its members' staff and facilities at the disposal of any and all government information agencies.[24] At the behest of Chester J. LaRoche, War Advertising Council chairman and vice president of Young & Rubicam, Inc., the graphics bureau of the government's Office of Facts and Figures (OFF) set up a National Advisory Council on Government Posters composed of prominent advertising-agency art directors. At an early meeting between OFF and its advisory admen, representatives of Young & Rubicam proposed to use survey research to establish a basis for effective poster design. Pursuing a style consistent with the commercial campaigns with which they were familiar, Y&R specialists undertook a "reaction survey" of thirty-three different war posters in Toronto, Canada between March 16 and April 1, 1942. Canada had been at war for more than two years as a member of the British Commonwealth, and had accumulated a significant catalog of war posters, which Y&R specialists used as evidence in favor of designing down to the lowest level of comprehension among the American public. Accordingly, Y&R's "reaction survey" revealed the Canadian public's "confusion" about certain posters' intent. Applying this lesson to the modeling of effective designs for American war posters, Y&R's specialists argued for a dramatic, yet straightforward style:

All war posters, no matter what they are, can help. But *good* war posters can do the job quicker and better. Anyone whose job it is to select war posters can be sure of getting only the most effective posters by asking two simple questions:

1. *Does the poster appeal to the emotions?*
2. *Is the poster a literal picture in photographic detail?*

The most effective war posters appeal to the emotions. No matter how beautiful the art work, how striking the colors, how clever the idea, unless a war poster appeals to a basic human emotion in both picture and text, it is not likely to make a deep impression.

The poster should be a picture, not an all-type poster or a symbolic design. And by a picture is meant a true and literal representation, in photographic detail, (though not necessarily a photograph) of people and objects as they are, and as they look to the millions of average people who make up the bulk of the population of the United States.

If it isn't a picture, it is not likely to make a powerful appeal. Abstract design and symbolism are to be avoided, as they are likely to be misunderstood or not understood at all.[25]

Young & Rubicam consultant George Gallup later concluded that an effective poster was one that could be understood by the "lower third" of the population. Reporting the results of the survey in *Art News,* a sympathetic commentator predicted that it "would not only be a guide for the production of (American) war posters now and advertising posters after the war, but for the 'fine' artist and the museum director to whom it would for the first time show what the public looks at."[26]

Further help in enforcing the advertising specialists' aversion to "abstract" posters came from a survey of war workers in five New Jersey plants. Focusing upon the posters of the Office for Emergency Management, survey data revealed that employees read Jean Carlu's worker holding a rivet gun as a gangster with a machine gun, and thought the poster's subject to be the FBI's war against crime. The same survey revealed that workers understood the stylized helmet of a German soldier in another Office for Emergency Management poster to represent the Liberty Bell, while other workers mistakenly believed "him" to be "the boss."[27]

Many specialists from the world of advertising considered the modeling of effective poster designs to be part of the much larger problem of communicating war information. They proposed that the government think of the effort to disseminate each war information theme as a "campaign." Well established in the commercial field, the campaign concept gained a toehold in the Office of Facts and Figures in early 1942, when William Bell and William B. Lewis encouraged director Archibald MacLeish to boil down quotations taken from President Roosevelt's annual congressional address "into

1941. OFFICE FOR EMERGENCY MANAGEMENT, DIVISION OF INFORMATION

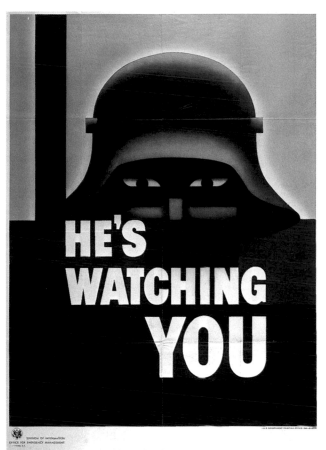

1942. OFFICE FOR EMERGENCY MANAGEMENT, DIVISION OF INFORMATION

LEFT | *Reconditioning of gas masks at the gas mask factory, Edgewood Arsenal, Maryland, June 1942*

Strong in the strength of the Lord we who fight in the people's cause will never stop until that cause is won

1942. U.S. OFFICE OF WAR INFORMATION

1778   1943

AMERICANS
will <u>always</u> fight for liberty

1943. U.S. OFFICE OF WAR INFORMATION

ABOVE | *Large poster after a painting by David Stone Martin issued by the Office of War Information and displayed in Union Station, Washington, D.C., December 1942*

one or two word campaign titles." "For example," Bell and Lewis explained, "the theme 'the President has called for a production program such as the nation has never ever attempted. It can be done and it will be done' and the quotation that goes with it both become 'Campaign—Work.'" Bell and Lewis complained that OFF's conception of its audience had been pitched far above the comprehension level of the man in the street, much less the man on the job. Noting OFF's tendency "to keep the psychological war on a plane far above the understanding of the people," Bell and Lewis explained:

> It would be wonderful indeed if the psychological war could be fought on an intellectual basis, if the American people who will win or lose this war were so educated and conditioned that we could bring them understanding on the terms we all prefer. But, through no fault of ours, they unfortunately are not so educated. And in pitting the strategy of truth against the strategy of terror, we cannot stop to educate—we must win a war. We must state the truth in terms that will be understood by all levels of intelligence. Further, we must dramatize the truth.[28]

Anticipating future criticism of the government's poster-making activities in the Office of War Information, Bell and Lewis concluded, "We may not approve the commercial philosophy of advertising agents, publicity men, or public relations experts but they all have highly developed mechanisms for informing the public. We believe these mechanisms should be used—and used fully—to tell the people the truth."[29]

To control the form of war messages, the government created the U.S. Office of War Information in June 1942. Among its responsibilities, OWI sought to review and approve the design and distribution of government posters. Eventually, contending groups within OWI clashed over poster design. While some embraced the poster as a demonstration of the practical value and utility of art, others valued it as evidence of the power of advertising. Both groups encouraged artists to derive their content from the themes and messages of government war information; however, those who saw posters as "war graphics" favored stylized images and symbolism, while recruits drawn from the world of advertising predictably wanted posters to be more like ads.

The necessity of poster coordination was clear to Francis E. Brennan, the former art director of *Fortune* magazine who became Chief of the OWI Graphics Division. Though Brennan's first statement on the subject of posters declared, "The essence of art is *freedom*," Brennan went on to note that "Until each [poster] is geared to a master procedure the total national impact will never be commensurate with the task before us—the people will never get a clear idea of what they are being asked to do, or who is asking them to do it."[30] Brennan's approach to the complexities of poster design had been the subject of a *Fortune* poster "portfolio" in August 1941. Sample posters commissioned from John C. Atherton, Carl Binder, Jean Carlu, and others demonstrated that though "cheap, efficient and pliant," the poster was "not a simple medium." Like the Office for Emergency Management's commissions and the winning entries of the MoMA poster competition, the designs in Brennan's portfolio were derived from collage, photomontage, and other fine-art sources. Brennan conceived a poster audience that had "matured" in the quarter-century between the First and Second World Wars, explaining that the American's "knowledge is greater, his background broader, his taste stricter. With rare exceptions the posters that moved him to lick the Kaiser would today do little more than arouse a strong nostalgia for the days when war was simple and unsubtle."[31] Seizing the main chance at OWI, Brennan proposed that posters be "war graphics," combining the sophisticated style of contemporary graphic design with the promotion of war aims.

Noting the individual efforts of the Navy Department, the Treasury, the Department of Agriculture, and the Office for Emergency Management as well as the efforts of business, industry, and relief organizations, OWI officials set out to coordinate the existing government poster output. Officials also determined to originate posters of their own design and to otherwise lead by example. Bearing the brunt of criticism of America's poster output, OWI officials tempered the ad hoc nature of poster procurement with instructions for artists. Over time OWI developed six war-information themes for its own internal use, as well as to guide other issuing agencies and major producers of mass-media entertainment. For example, future senator Alan Cranston, then chief of OWI's Foreign Language Division, described for Walt Disney Studios "six basic propaganda themes" developed as background for "general information programs":

N.D. RUSSIAN WAR RELIEF, INC.

[2] The Nature of our Allies—the United Nations theme, our close ties with Britain, Russia and China, Mexicans and Americans fighting side by side on Bataan and on the battle-fronts.

1943. U.S. OFFICE OF WAR INFORMATION

1943. U.S. ARMY DEPARTMENT

1943. U.S. OFFICE OF WAR INFORMATION

[1] The Nature of the Enemy—general or detailed descriptions of this enemy, such as, he hates religion, persecutes labor, kills Jews and other minorities, smashes home life, debases women, etc.

1943. U.S. NAVY DEPARTMENT, INCENTIVE DIVISION

[3] The Need to Work—the countless ways in which Americans must work if we are to win the war, in factories, on ships, in mines, in fields, etc.

[4] The Need to Fight—the need for fearless waging of war on land, sea, and skies, with bullets, bombs, bare hands, if we are to win.

1943. U.S. NAVY DEPARTMENT, INCENTIVE DIVISION

1943. U.S. OFFICE OF WAR INFORMATION

FOOD IS A WEAPON

DON'T WASTE IT !
BUY WISELY - COOK CAREFULLY - EAT IT ALL

FOLLOW THE NATIONAL WARTIME NUTRITION PROGRAM

1943. U.S. OFFICE OF WAR INFORMATION

[5] The Need to Sacrifice— Americans are willing to give up all luxuries, devote all spare time to the war effort, etc., to help win the war.

When you ride ALONE you ride with Hitler !

Join a Car-Sharing Club TODAY !

1943, UNATTRIBUTED

USE IT UP – WEAR IT OUT – *MAKE IT DO!*

OUR LABOR AND OUR GOODS ARE FIGHTING

1943. U.S. OFFICE OF WAR INFORMATION

Keep America ROLLING!

**Save your 5 best TIRES
Sell others to Uncle Sam**

1942. OFFICE FOR EMERGENCY MAN-
AGEMENT, DIVISION OF INFORMATION

IS YOUR TRIP NECESSARY?

NEEDLESS TRAVEL
interferes with the War Effort

1943. OFFICE OF DEFENSE TRANSPORTATION, U.S.
OFFICE OF WAR INFORMATION

Keep us flying!

BUY WAR BONDS

OFFICIAL U. S. TREASURY POSTER

1943. U.S. TREASURY DEPARTMENT

ABOVE | *Extending the Treasury's goal of universal war-bond ownership to new audiences, this poster pictured one member of an elite corps of Black airmen. The model, Robert Deiz, had recently joined the 99th Pursuit Squadron of Black aviators established at Tuskeegee College in the spring of 1942. Deiz went on to fly ninety-three successful missions with the 99th over North Africa and Italy, including several in which he downed German Luftwaffe aircraft in his P-40 Tomahawk.*[33]

[6] The Americans—we are fighting for the four freedoms, the principles of the Atlantic Charter, Democracy, and no discrimination against races and religions, etc.[32]

THE Atlantic Charter

THE President of THE UNITED STATES OF AMERICA and the Prime Minister, Mr. *Churchill*, representing HIS MAJESTY'S GOVERNMENT IN THE UNITED KINGDOM, being met together, deem it right to make known certain common principles in the national policies of their respective countries on which they base their hopes for a better future for the world.

1. *Their countries seek no aggrandizement, territorial or other.*

2. *They desire to see no territorial changes that do not accord with the freely expressed wishes of the peoples concerned.*

3. *They respect the right of all peoples to choose the form of government under which they will live; and they wish to see sovereign rights and self-government restored to those who have been forcibly deprived of them.*

4. *They will endeavor, with due respect for their existing obligations, to further the enjoyment by all States, great or small, victor or vanquished, of access, on equal terms, to the trade and to the raw materials of the world which are needed for their economic prosperity.*

5. *They desire to bring about the fullest collaboration between all nations in the economic field with the object of securing, for all, improved labor standards, economic advancement and social security.*

6. *After the final destruction of the Nazi tyranny, they hope to see established a peace which will afford to all nations the means of dwelling*

in safety within their own boundaries, and which will afford assurance that all the men in all the lands may live out their lives in freedom from fear and want.

7. *Such a peace should enable all men to traverse the high seas and oceans without hindrance.*

8. *They believe that all of the nations of the world, for realistic as well as spiritual reasons, must come to the abandonment of the use of force. Since no future peace can be maintained if land, sea or air armaments continue to be employed by nations which threaten, or may threaten, aggression outside of their frontiers, they believe, pending the establishment of a wider and permanent system of general security, that the disarmament of such nations is essential. They will likewise aid and encourage all other practicable measures which will lighten for peace-loving peoples the crushing burden of armaments.*

FRANKLIN D. ROOSEVELT

WINSTON S. CHURCHILL.

August 14, 1941

1943. U.S. OFFICE OF WAR INFORMATION

SAVE FREEDOM OF SPEECH

BUY WAR BONDS

SAVE FREEDOM OF WORSHIP

EACH ACCORDING TO THE DICTATES
OF HIS OWN CONSCIENCE

BUY WAR BONDS

OURS...to fight for

FREEDOM FROM WANT

ALL: 1943. U.S. OFFICE OF WAR
INFORMATION

*Setting out to "do something bigger than a war poster," illustrator
Norman Rockwell prepared these images interpreting the Four
Freedoms enumerated in President Roosevelt's annual congressional
address January 6, 1941, and outlined in the Atlantic Charter
jointly issued by President Roosevelt and British Prime Minister
Winston Churchill August 14, 1941. Using his Vermont neighbors as
models, Rockwell prepared a series of rough poster sketches that he
offered to OWI. Rockwell later recalled that OWI's "man in charge
of posters" dismissed the proposal, with the explanation that OWI
sought the work of "real artists" rather than illustrators. Rockwell's
finished paintings eventually appeared in four consecutive issues of
the* Saturday Evening Post *in February and March 1943, and
went on to become some of the most widely-reproduced images of the
era. In 1943 the Treasury mounted a traveling exhibition of the
paintings on behalf of bond sales, and reproduced the images in
posters as well.[34]*

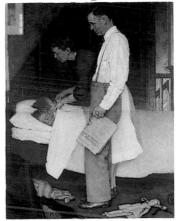

OURS...to fight for

FREEDOM FROM FEAR

HELP BRING THEM BACK TO YOU!

Find time for war work

Raise and share food

Walk and carry packages

Conserve everything you have

Save 10% in War Bonds

THIS IS A
V
HOME

MAKE YOURS
A VICTORY HOME!

1943. U.S. OFFICE OF WAR INFORMATION

The suspicions of a conservative Congress helped OWI's volunteer admen consolidate their position within the agency. Many in Congress viewed OWI's domestic branch as little more than a publicity mill for New Deal propaganda. Subsequent cuts in funding for 1943 domestic information activities had a direct impact upon what posters looked like and talked about. Henceforth, the overall dramatization of American war aims played out in demonstrations of commercial techniques and effects.

Advertising's critics, then and now, have questioned the use of such techniques to "sell" the war. Some noted the political context of the advertising industry's "private war," which disarmed critics and forestalled government regulation. Despite an absence of consumer products to sell during the war, the advertising industry prospered. The Roosevelt administration granted "good will" advertising protected status as a tax-deductible business expense. Emanating from the War Advertising Council and the Office of War Information, skilled demonstrations of advertising techniques were a powerful means of preserving the commercial viability of the mass media, as a channel for communicating government war information to the public.[35]

OWI information campaigns used posters in concert with magazines, radio, and other kinds of paid space donated to the government through the auspices of the War Advertising Council. The results were sometimes oddly superficial—posters that translated messages of sacrifice and struggle into the familiar advertising world of smiling faces and carefree households. In a bureaucratic skirmish that has since loomed large in the historiography of American advertising, a group of OWI writers resigned their positions rather than accept the new sensibility. At issue were posters about ordering coal early; "V-Homes"; a poster headlined: "I'm Happy in my new war job"; and another picturing a young girl and her mother, captioned: "We'll have lots to eat this winter, won't we mother?"[36]

N.D. U.S. OFFICE OF WAR INFORMATION

OWI Graphics Bureau chief Francis Brennan, the man who had brought modern art to *Fortune* magazine, joined the writers in tendering his resignation to OWI director Elmer Davis. Brennan found it "absurd" that OWI's advertising professionals trimmed poster content to fit commercial channels of poster distribution, particularly to retail stores. "Some advertising techniques are valuable," Brennan wrote in his resignation letter to Davis. "If…you mean the fairly simple job of getting messages printed, distributed, and read, I agree. But, if you mean psychological approaches, content, and ideas, I most firmly do not agree. In my opinion those techniques have done more toward dimming perceptions, suspending critical values, and spreading the sticky syrup of complacency over the people than almost any other factor in the complex pattern of our supercharged lives."[37]

Advertising specialists who rejected the esoteric qualities of Brennan's "war graphics" completed the consolidation of government poster design. Facing the budget ax wielded by a conservative Congress, OWI ceased to be an originating point for posters and became instead a coordinating point for the poster work of other war agencies. In September 1943, OWI invoked for the first time its authority to enforce standards upon all government posters for quality, mechanical specifications, quantity, and distribution.[38]

Conforming to the realities of a limited budget for domestic operations, OWI maintained a skeleton poster-layout staff in Washington headed by Jacques DunLany, the agency's new graphics bureau chief, and appointed James D. Herbert as New York liaison to an all-volunteer Art Directors Pool. The inspiration of War Advertising Council chairman Chester J. LaRoche, this "Art Pool" formalized the working relationship between the government agencies using posters and the advertising-agency art directors who now designed them. Determined to put the procurement of government poster design on a "business basis," DunLany and Herbert

N.D. U.S. NAVY DEPARTMENT,
INCENTIVE DIVISION

1943. U.S. OFFICE OF WAR INFORMATION

1944. DISTRIBUTED FOR THE ISSUING
AGENCIES BY OWI

ended the practice of soliciting speculative sketches and participating in poster competitions. OWI began to make token payments to commercial illustrators for paintings assigned by the Art Pool as an "earnest of serious intent." OWI's Washington office sorted the problems and poster requests of the Army, the Navy, the FBI, the Treasury, the War Production Board, the Office of Defense Transportation, and the Maritime Commission. Meanwhile, the creative work of poster design was relocated to the meeting rooms of the Art Directors Club of New York. "We needed artists . . . and artists of

unquestioned standing," DunLany recalled. "There had been too many false starts, too many posters ordered on whims, too many people with a new layout idea of 'V for Victory' or some other well meaning but ambiguous theme that would never garner an extra pound of fat or sell a single war bond." By February 1945, officials proudly noted that the process of poster procurement had been reduced to three months: one month for layout, a second for production, and a third for distribution.[39]

This was one of only a handful of unsolicited poster designs used by a government agency. Submitted by artist Wesley Heyman (described by one OWI Art Pool member as a "comparative 'unknown'"), the image of a spaniel and a gold star—designating the loss of a loved one—"coincided both with a need and a poster-committee decision to produce a human-interest 'change-of-pace' design." In addition to being printed as a poster, the image was reproduced in black-and-white and color in employee magazines, Sunday newspaper supplements, and other publications. OWI officials figured that its "aggregate reproduction was in the millions," noting that "requests for it broke all previous records."[40]

...*because somebody talked!*

1944. DISTRIBUTED FOR THE ISSUING AGENCIES BY OWI

1943. U.S. OFFICE OF DEFENSE TRANSPORTATION

1944. U.S. OFFICE OF DEFENSE TRANSPORTATION

1943. U.S. TREASURY DEPARTMENT

Poster-campaign guidelines for the Treasury's Sixth, Seventh and Eighth War Loans during 1944–1945 reveal how the procurement process worked. Receiving the Treasury's poster request, Art Pool chairman Elwood Whitney, vice-president and art director of Foote, Cone & Belding, convened a meeting with representatives of the Treasury,

participating members of the Art Pool, and their fellow copywriters. The art directors and copywriters discussed the campaign and its stated goal, and exchanged information on posters that the Treasury had found successful in the past. For example, Treasury officials believed that posters conveying a "personal appeal" worked best—such as the image of a soldier throwing a grenade captioned "Let 'Em Have It" and the image of a GI waving from a porthole, captioned "Till we meet again."[41]

Discussion also focused upon images and copy appeals that the Treasury wished to avoid, such as the theme "Bring him back sooner," which OWI's Herbert noted could be misinterpreted by the public as an official "promise" of a loved one's safe return. The Treasury also banished casualty images of the kind used in OWI's own "careless talk" posters. Art Pool member Gordon Aymar of Compton Advertising reported to Herbert, "We were warned not to go to extremes of blood and guts—no mutilation pictures." "Strange as it may seem," Aymar wrote, "[the Treasury's representatives] stated that the American public did not like to face the fact that their bond money was going to kill Japs. As an example of this, posters showing bloody scenes of an American bayoneting a Jap soldier didn't get anywhere. On the other hand American soldiers in danger of being bayoneted by Japs apparently did the trick."[42] The art directors had their work cut out for them. Herbert replied, "We are forced to establish direct and personal relationship with the boy fighting at the front and not show any scenes of mutilation or death. Perhaps you can find a way to suggest all this and not actually show the ultimate tragedy. If anyone can find a way, you can."[43]

BUY WAR BONDS

1942. U.S. TREASURY DEPARTMENT

1944. DISTRIBUTED FOR ISSUING AGENCIES
BY U.S. OFFICE OF WAR INFORMATION

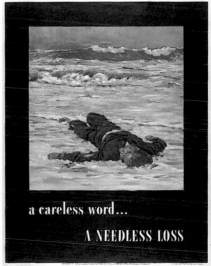

1943. U.S. OFFICE OF WAR INFORMATION

BUY THAT INVASION BOND!

1944. U.S. TREASURY DEPARTMENT

OFFICIAL U.S. TREASURY POSTER

1944. U.S. TREASURY DEPARTMENT

1944. U.S. TREASURY DEPARTMENT

N.D. UNATTRIBUTED

Posters publicizing the Treasury's Sixth War Loan sought to prevent a decline in war bond purchases anticipated with the surrender of Germany. The subsequent poster campaign urged Americans to "keep on buying" while shifting the focus of attack from Europe to the Pacific.

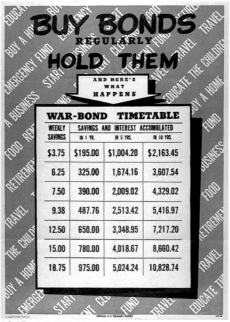

WAR-BOND TIMETABLE			
WEEKLY SAVINGS	SAVINGS AND INTEREST ACCUMULATED		
	IN 1 YR.	IN 5 YRS.	IN 10 YRS.
$3.75	$195.00	$1,004.20	$2,163.45
6.25	325.00	1,674.16	3,607.54
7.50	390.00	2,009.02	4,329.02
9.38	487.76	2,513.42	5,416.97
12.50	650.00	3,348.95	7,217.20
15.00	780.00	4,018.67	8,660.42
18.75	975.00	5,024.24	10,828.74

1945. U.S. TREASURY DEPARTMENT

1944. U.S. TREASURY DEPARTMENT

Treasury policy banned battlefield casualty images, but not necessarily battlefield scenes. Posters publicizing the Seventh and Eighth war loans dramatized the "selfish reasons for buying bonds" and the "inequity of sacrifice between the home front and the fighting front."[44]

The ascension of the Art Pool in OWI affected the appearance of government war posters. Gone was the esthetic of "war graphics." In its place stood the conventions of commercial illustration. Predicated upon ready accessibility to the lower third of the American population, commercial illustration rejected symbolism and abstract images for literal representation and emotional pull. If, as critics charged, turning over poster design to Madison Avenue art directors made government posters as bland and inoffensive as advertising, in most instances this was in fact what OWI's poster clients desired: a selective reality of sacrifice and struggle exorcised of troublesome detail. While many advertising specialists had predicted the diminution of their industry with America's entry into the war, precisely the opposite had occurred.[45] Government information in general and government posters in particular became highly modeled and nuanced. Though not a medium of commercial promotion at the beginning of the war, the poster returned to prominence as a powerful device for the selling of social, economic, and political ideas.

CARE is costly

BUY AND HOLD WAR BONDS

ALL: 1945. U.S. TREASURY DEPARTMENT

7th WAR LOAN NOW··ALL TOGETHER

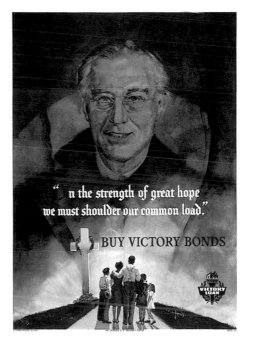

" n the strength of great hope we must shoulder our common load."

BUY VICTORY BONDS

VICTORY LOAN

RIGHT | *After the death of President Roosevelt on April 12, 1945, the Treasury issued this poster as a memorial.*

Change of shift, Reynolds Alloys Company, Sheffield, Alabama, August 1942

CHAPTER FOUR

RETOOLING FOR VICTORY: THE FACTORY FLOOR

World War II industrial incentive posters traditionally have been interpreted as visualizations of wartime cooperation between labor and business. But when placed in their historical context, these posters reveal tensions between workers and management that were, like the posters themselves, ever-present. The government agencies and businesses that created these images did so not to celebrate a new working relationship, but to overcome deep-seated problems in defense factories that threatened conversion to wartime production. Government planners hoped that through public-relation campaigns that relied heavily on posters, they would create an atmosphere of urgency, participation, and factory discipline.

From the perspective of government officials, the period leading up to World War II was a time of great uncertainty. The country lingered in a depression that was only just beginning to recede due to increased defense spending. The nation's factories were old and out of date, and many companies held back from plunging too deeply into defense production, fearful that the war would end before they could realize profits on their investments. Violent conflict appeared to be the norm in industrial relations, as workers battled company guards and police in their effort to establish union representation. From 1933 to 1938, Americans had witnessed unprecedented labor unrest, as over 5,600,000 workers participated in more than 10,000 strikes.[46] In negotiations between management and labor, distrust, if not unbridled hatred, characterized the participants' attitudes toward those who sat across the bargaining table.

As America's entry into the war drew closer, the battle for unionization of industry heated up. In 1940, Philip Murray, President of the Congress of Industrial Organizations (CIO), announced to the executive board, "I tell you I don't give a tinker's damn about national defense interfering with our work. I feel that we ought to go ahead just the same as if that kind of situation were not in our midst. Organize and fight and do the job as we originally intended to do five years ago."[47] In the end of 1940 and throughout 1941, labor waged a new series of organizing campaigns in the auto, steel, airplane, heavy-equipment, and coal-mining industries—the very heart of the defense industries. In 1941, there were more than 4,000 strikes involving more than 2 million workers, approximately 6 percent of the entire labor force of the country.[48] This wave of strikes added more than 1.5 million new union members, an increase of about 17 percent, and brought membership to an all-time high of around 10.5 million workers.[49]

Most labor and business leaders recognized that soon public opinion would not tolerate anything less than the appearance of their total cooperation with the war effort. In public-relations campaigns that intensified in the months leading up to America's formal entrance into the war, both labor and business strove to demonstrate their commitment and willingness to sacrifice. Through posters and other media, labor and business put aside any reluctance they might have felt and crafted their own patriotic image.

During the defense emergency of the early 1940s, for example, the National Association of Manufacturers, a trade association with long experience in the poster field—and a record of intractable opposition to even the most minor

1942. NATIONAL ASSOCIATION OF MANUFACTURERS

adjustments of capitalism under the New Deal—distributed a series by illustrator McClelland Barclay. Each poster in this series presented a syllogism of national purpose and private enterprise, culminating with "Defense of our liberty begins in the factory." Each also featured a small inset depicting the harmonious organization of work represented by knowing managers and willing workers.

ALL: 1942. NATIONAL ASSOCIATION OF MANUFACTURERS

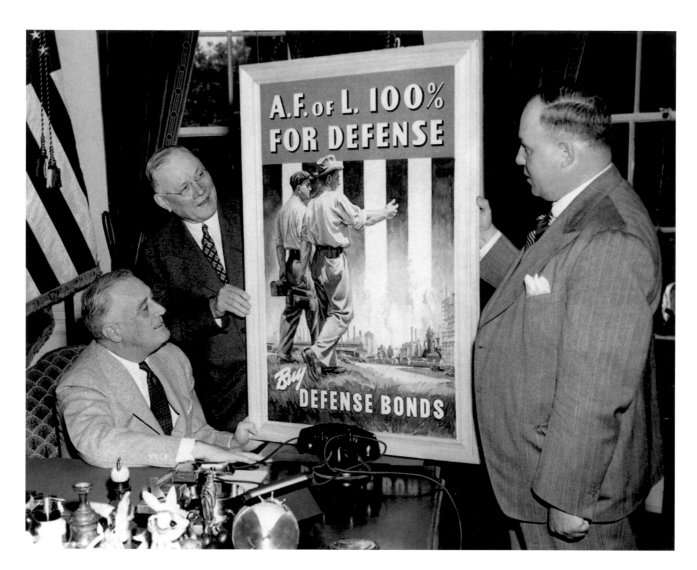

AFL president William Green and secretary-treasurer George Meany presenting President Roosevelt with a newly issued AFL defense-bond poster, 1941

CA. 1944. AMERICAN FEDERATION OF LABOR

N.D. CONGRESS OF INDUSTRIAL ORGANIZATIONS

SUPPORT THE RED CROSS
NATIONAL CIO WAR RELIEF COMMITTEE

N.D. CONGRESS OF INDUSTRIAL ORGANIZATIONS

Give!

A·F of L supports
RED CROSS
LABOR LEAGUE FOR HUMAN RIGHTS
UNITED NATIONS RELIEF-A.F.of l

1944. AMERICAN FEDERATION OF LABOR

The American Federation of Labor (AFL) and the CIO made it clear that they would not fall behind business in demonstrations of nationalism. Each union geared up its communications department to produce posters urging their members to support the government's defense effort in all ways possible. Immediately following President Roosevelt's declaration of war on December 8, 1941, both the AFL and the CIO declared their total support for the war effort. They announced a no-strike pledge and a commitment to work toward full 24-hour production.[50]

Many of the nation's largest industrial corporations engaged their unions in public-relations contests leading to claims and counterclaims. The case of General Motors (GM) and the United Auto Workers (UAW) was significant, because many businesses followed the tenor and tone of GM's public- and employee-relations practices. In the spring of 1942, GM learned that the UAW had prepared an advertisement attributing the auto industry's war-production achievements to labor, and specifically to UAW's plan for wartime conversion. Literally overnight GM prepared an advertisement entitled "Good News from the Production Front" that ran nationally the next day. The GM advertisement undercut the UAW's claim and set in motion the company's wartime public-relations campaign. GM's advertisements sought to erase from public memory the corporation's reluctant support of early defense efforts by demonstrating its willingness to sacrifice all for the war. Campbell-Ewald, the advertising agency that prepared the response and advised GM during the war, proudly summed up its wartime approach in 1950: "The paradox created is this: That by generous cooperation with government and skillful attunement to the popularized sentiments, business helps government in the long run to defeat itself in the continuing effort to control business."[51]

1942. OLDSMOBILE DIVISION, GENERAL MOTORS CORPORATION

In 1942, GM's Oldsmobile division (which had converted its manufacturing facilities to aircraft production) ran a series of shop-floor posters projecting themes of participation, sacrifice, and shared responsibility. Its overall message proclaimed GM's commitment to the government's war effort, and called on its employees to do the same.

ALL: 1942. OLDSMOBILE DIVISION, GENERAL
MOTORS CORPORATION

IDEA?   IDEA?

IDEA?

IDEA?

IDEA?

IDEAS WILL HELP
BEAT THE PROMISE
LET'S HAVE YOURS!

ALL: 1942. RCA MANUFACTURING COMPANY

HELP RCA HELP USA

YOU AND I

BEAT THE PROMISE

Many war contractors sought to instill a sense of urgency among workers at the scene of production. RCA Manufacturing Corporation linked the company's identity and production to national interests quite literally. For its "Beat the Promise" campaign, which referred to surpassing established war-production quotas, RCA sent out representatives with recording equipment to interview former employees serving in the military. The company then played the recordings over speakers installed in its plants to help reinforce the posters' messages.[52]

ALL: 1942. RCA MANUFACTURING COMPANY

The wartime emergency required that industry do more than just shift its production from consumer goods to war material and increase productivity. To guarantee a reliable supply of armaments, the conversion also demanded a fundamental change in workers' and managers' attitudes—from antagonism to cooperation. The War Department, the War Production Board, and other government offices launched a concerted promotional campaign urging workers and managers to take personal responsibility and make individual sacrifices to win the war. Individual companies and labor unions followed suit.

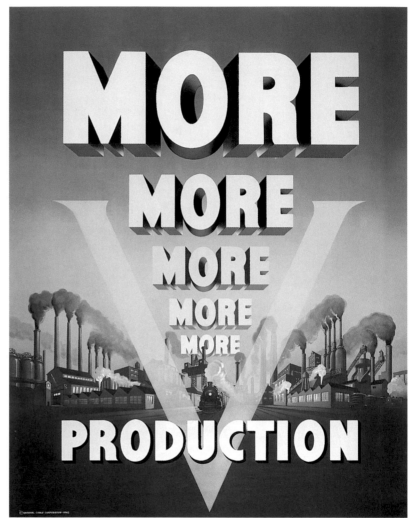

1942. GENERAL CABLE CORPORATION

CA. 1942. NATIONAL CIO WAR RELIEF COMMITTEE

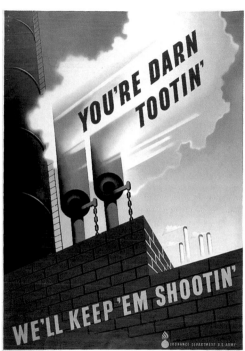

1942. U.S. ARMY, ORDNANCE DEPARTMENT

Women inspecting drill bits in an unidentified Midwest tool company, August 1942

War Production Board posters brought the urgency of the war onto the factory floor. Tacked up on bulletin boards, next to time clocks, on factory walls, and in break rooms, these posters served as a constant reminder of the war and the need to increase production. The poster as a medium was imbued with attributes that made it ideal for carrying these messages, and for expressing both the war's material needs and its democratic aims. The S. D. Warren Company (a paper manu-facturer) described the need for posters, stating in a promotional publication: "Earnest, striving men and women must be stirred to enlarge their capacities for effort. Efficient workers must be helped to attain even greater efficiency. And these objectives must be gained by methods that are in harmony with the principles of a democratic society; they cannot be gained by commanding them; they must be gained by supplying incentives that will induce voluntary action."[53]

Kinda give it your personal attention, will you?

MORE PRODUCTION

ALL: N.D. WAR PRODUCTION BOARD

She's a swell plane– give us more!

MORE PRODUCTION

He's a fighting fool give him the best you've got

MORE PRODUCTION

MEN WORKING TOGETHER!

1941. U.S. OFFICE FOR EMERGENCY MANAGEMENT, DIVISION OF INFORMATION

Series after series of posters directed employees to get to work—anything less was tantamount to treason. Employers did not necessarily expect their work forces to take all poster slogans literally. Rather, businesses placed these displays at the scene of production to create an atmosphere of unity and urgency. Posters called upon workers to conserve, keep their breaks short, and follow their supervisors' instructions. Their main thrust was to convince workers, many of whom participated in the violent labor conflicts of the 1930s, that they were no longer just employees of GM or U.S. Steel, but rather Uncle Sam's "production soldiers" on the industrial front line of the war.[54]

The shift in perspective from employee to production soldier was tied exclusively to the wartime emergency. Posters were important tools in creating an environment that helped create this shift in attitude without changing industries' management structures. Although posters carried many direct messages to work harder, keep quiet, or conserve, the underlying and more important message that was repeated hundreds of times over was the relationship of production to patriotism, and the transformation of employees into factory combatants.

ALL: 1942. FISHER BODY DIVISION, GENERAL MOTORS CORPORATION

Steelworkers on break at Pittsburg Works, Columbia Steel Company (a division of United States Steel), Pittsburg, California, ca. 1943. On the panel next to the men is the following text: "This piece of an American warship was struck by a Japanese bomb or shell. On the day that you were absent from work. This is war. You are a production soldier. Your duty is to be on your job. Don't be absent as long as you are physically able to work. If there is no work on your regular job accept work that is always available on other jobs. Production soldiers don't desert the fighting. Keep your work attendance record 100%. War Production Drive Committee."

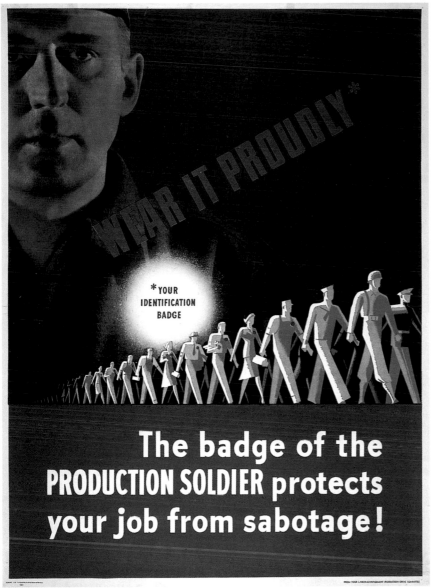

1942, MAGILL-WEINSHEIMER COMPANY

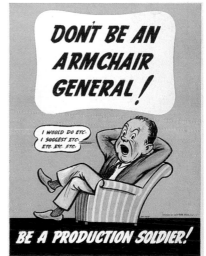

1942, MAGILL-WEINSHEIMER COMPANY

1942, HARRIS, SEYBOLD, POTTER COMPANY

ALL: 1942. WALTER KIDDE & COMPANY, INC.

Absent from posters were any direct or implied messages that hard work would result in personal or company gain. The motivating force to encourage greater employee commitment was purely patriotic duty. If patriotism was not enough, many of the posters played very directly on the guilt of those who, for whatever reason, were not in the military.

The posters reminded workers that if they were not risking their lives on the battlefield, the least they could do was keep their bathroom breaks short. This coupling of patriotism and guilt presented businesses, through their graphic-art departments, with ample subject material to spin out countless illustrations designed to instill factory discipline.

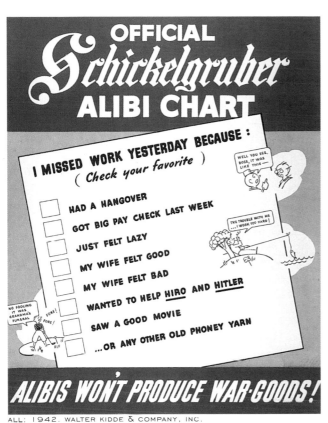

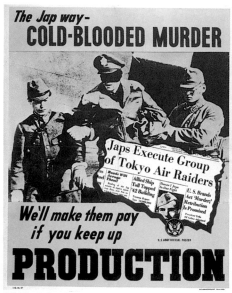

1943. U.S. ARMY DEPARTMENT

N.D. UNATTRIBUTED

1942, MAGILL-WEINSHEIMER COMPANY

1943, NORTH AMERICAN AVIATION

1942, NATIONAL PROCESS
COMPANY

1943, U.S. NAVY DEPARTMENT,
INCENTIVE DIVISION

ALL: 1942. PRODUCED FOR JOINT
LABOR-MANAGEMENT WAR PRODUCTION
DRIVE COMMITTEE BY ROGERS, KELLOGG,
STILLSON, INC.

To help facilitate a new era of labor-management relations, on March 2, 1942, Donald M. Nelson, director of the War Production Board, called for companies to voluntarily establish joint labor-management committees.[55] Nelson opposed giving union leaders a role in industrial planning. He did, however, reluctantly accept the idea that labor could play a part in increasing productivity. The labor-management committees were to focus on increasing production on the shop floor, encouraging suggestions from workers, eliminating rejects, advocating conservation, reducing absenteeism, and promoting tool care and safety.[56] About five thousand companies registered committees, covering about seven million employees, but many of these met only once or twice.

Approximately three thousand committees actually functioned at a time. About half limited their activities to bond drives and war propaganda, and only a small number actually met to improve production.[57]

In promoting these committees, T. K. Quinn, Director General of the War Production Drive, tied their existence to larger American principles and war aims. "To deny this opportunity is in effect to deny the principles of freedom and democracy." He went on to write: "A labor-management Committee in a Nazi or Jap factory is unthinkable as it is admirable in one of ours." To sell the labor-management committee idea to businesses, Quinn repeatedly assured them that the committees would not encroach on managerial preroga-

1942. THE EMPLOYER'S LIABILITY ASSURANCE
CORPORATION, LTD.

1943. U.S. NAVY DEPARTMENT, INCENTIVE DIVISION

tives. He stated, "Any talk or fear of labor wanting to replace management is largely nonsense. Labor knows that management should be a reward of ability and special training. Labor is intensely proud, we believe, of being labor."[58] In essence labor-management committees functioned within the narrow range that management permitted. Nelson of the WPB made it clear that the purpose of the committees was to increase productivity and boost morale, not to "put labor into management…or management into labor."[59]

One of the principal functions of labor-management committees was arranging for a steady display of production-incentive posters throughout plants. The committees obtained posters from a variety of sources that included WPB cata-

logues, private publishers such as Rogers, Kellogg, Stillson, Inc., and the art departments of their own companies. Most poster images left little question as to the difference between production soldiers and their officers. Business leaders did not intend the new team approach to give workers a role in managerial areas of planning and oversight. Even if artists depicted workers with heroic attributes and symbolized labor as a muscular giant, posters nonetheless conveyed the message that workers' contribution lay in providing physical strength and technical skill.

The posters produced by the Briggs Manufacturing Company's labor-management committee fit comfortably into the narrow confines of maintaining employee discipline. Posters castigated workers for punching in late, taking long breaks, damaging the company's equipment, and even drinking after work. Artists turned what had been considered common infractions against the company into acts of betrayal, murder, and disloyalty against the nation.

ALL: 1942. THE JOINT LABOR-MANAGEMENT COMMITTEE OF BRIGGS MANUFACTURING COMPANY

SHOOTIN' THE BULL AINT SHOOTIN' NAZIS!

THE JOINT LABOR-MANAGEMENT COMMITTEE OF BRIGGS MANUFACTURING COMPANY

NO MORE SMOKES FOR HIM!

Were You To Blame?

THE JOINT LABOR-MANAGEMENT COMMITTEE OF BRIGGS MANUFACTURING COMPANY

ALL: 1942. THE JOINT LABOR-MANAGEMENT COMMITTEE OF BRIGGS MANUFACTURING COMPANY

DID You BREAK THIS MILLING CUTTER?

IT WILL TAKE 80 DAYS TO REPLACE!

THE JOINT LABOR-MANAGEMENT COMMITTEE OF BRIGGS MANUFACTURING COMPANY

The posters of J. Howard Miller for the labor-management committee at the Westinghouse Electric and Manufacturing Company are good examples of how companies blended traditional themes of workplace discipline with the imagery of sacrifice and patriotism. Many of the images implied a newly entrusted work force, however, this empowerment was narrowly defined. While the now-famous poster of a woman with raised arm proclaimed "We Can Do It!," other Westinghouse posters clarified what "It" meant. The committee primarily encouraged these women and their fellow workmen to follow orders and work harder. For employees who wondered about their role in production another of Miller's posters provided the answer. This time a friendly manager counseled, "Any Questions About Your Work?....Ask Your Supervisor."

Although new cooperative relationships in industry between management and labor helped to win the war, American business leaders successfully resisted lasting efforts to restructure basic relationships in the workplace. While 80 percent of the managers felt that the labor-management committees had helped in the war effort, fewer than 10 percent retained them by 1948.[60] With the end of the war, the production soldiers in essence also received their discharge papers. With no lasting change in employee-management relations, the struggle between labor and business resumed. In 1946, labor unrest surpassed all previous years, with 4,990 reported strikes involving approximately 4,600,000 employees, around 10.5 percent of the work force.[61]

N.D. WESTINGHOUSE WAR PRODUCTION CO-ORDINATING COMMITTEE

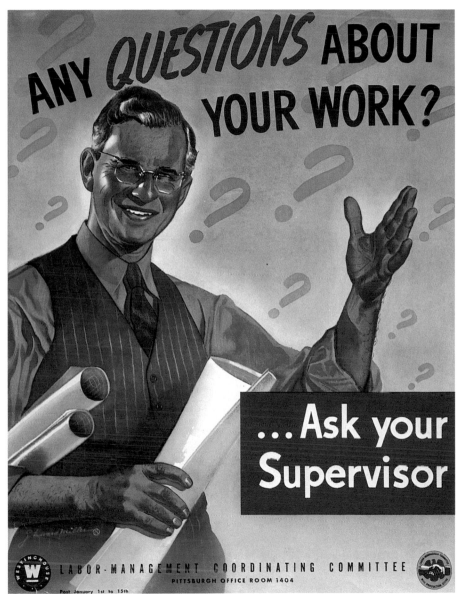

N.D. WESTINGHOUSE LABOR-MANAGEMENT
COORDINATING COMMITTEE

N.D. WESTINGHOUSE WAR PRODUCTION CO-ORDINATING COMMITTEE

You too,
would want
the best!

LET'S BE OUR OWN INSPECTORS

POST SEPT. 1ST TO 15TH. WAR PRODUCTION CO-ORDINATING COMMITTEE

N.D. WESTINGHOUSE WAR PRODUCTION CO-ORDINATING COMMITTEE

EMPLOYMENT
DEPT.

Do what you can to
help Returning Veterans

N.D. WESTINGHOUSE HEADQUARTERS
INDUSTRIAL RELATIONS

This is America..

Where a fellow can start on the home team and wind up in the big league. Where there is always room at the top for the fellow who has it on the ball ★ *This is your America!*

...Keep it Free!

CHAPTER FIVE

POSTWAR AIMS AND PRIVATE ASPIRATIONS

Whether created by government or corporations, the poster on the home front conveyed social, economic, and political ideas through imagery. Throughout the war, the imagery on such posters celebrated the middle-class home, the traditional nuclear family, consumerism, and free enterprise. Pictures of men and women conveyed assumptions about the roles of each in victory, and offered a vision of life in an ideal postwar world.

The Sheldon-Claire Company of Chicago, one of several private poster publishers, successfully structured its World War II material not only to meet wartime demands but to satisfy corporate sensibilities as well. Founded in the 1920s, the company developed a distinctive style of bold, colorful graphics and simple copy. At the outset of the war, Sheldon-Claire shifted the focus of its employee-incentive posters from motivating salesmen to inspiring production workers. Over the next three years, Sheldon-Claire produced five poster series: "Produce for Victory," "This is America," "Keep It Free," "Stay on the Job," "Your Job is Vital to Victory," and "The American Way Works." Sold in sets of approximately thirty posters each, the company intended buyers to display a different poster each week for the length of series. Clients ranged from small to large firms, including Carnegie-Illinois Steel Corporation, which purchased five hundred sets of the series "Produce for Victory."

"America is great because liberty-loving Americans have made it great. You've got to <u>want</u> <u>freedom</u> to work for it — to fight for it — to die for it."

PRODUCE FOR VICTORY!

"No nation of slaves can match a nation of free men. We're doing more because <u>we want to</u> than they can because <u>they have to!</u>"

PRODUCE FOR VICTORY!

"*WE*, the Americans of today, know our duty to the Americans of yesterday and the Americans of tomorrow. *WE* shall keep the fires of freedom burning."

PRODUCE FOR VICTORY!

ALL: 1942. THE SHELDON-CLAIRE COMPANY

The Sheldon-Claire company claimed that its World War II posters embraced several innovative communication techniques. A company newsletter later asserted that its designers intended the posters to respond to the needs of the moment rather than to general managerial concerns. They created the wartime series "to be objective....No longer designed to disseminate management propaganda," and aimed the material at both management and employees. Sheldon-Claire also believed that it had successfully improved the material appeal of the poster medium. The company stated: "The wartime series featured emotional appeals—for the first time. The preaching of the 1920s and the rational and intellectual appeals of the 1930s yielded to a poster design and copy style that was based on fact, but which was designed primarily to influence the emotions of employees."[62]

Each series maintained a uniform design, coupling the work of a well-known photojournalist with positive motivational copy. In colorized portraits and idealized scenes of American life, sympathetic images created a patriotic rationale for the war. "This is America," a series of thirty-one posters produced in 1942, put forth an array of reasons for personal participation during the national emergency. The series also established a narrative that included not only what the nation sought to defend, but also what it would need to preserve in postwar America. It accomplished this task by interweaving commonly accepted political values such as freedom of religion and speech with traditional representations of the nuclear family and images of national abundance, personal opportunity, and free enterprise.

This is America..

. . . where every boy can dream of being President. Where free schools, free opportunity, free enterprise, have built the most decent nation on earth. A nation built upon the rights of all men ★ *This is your America*

...Keep it Free!

ALL: 1942. THE SHELDON-CLAIRE COMPANY

This is America..

. . . a nation with more homes, more motor cars, more telephones–more comforts than any nation on earth. Where free workers and free enterprise are building a better world for all people ★ *This is your America*

...Keep it Free!

This is America..

...where the family is a sacred institution. Where children love, honor and respect their parents ...where a man's home is his castle ★ *This is your America*

...Keep it Free!

This is America..

...industrial center of the world...maker of steel...miller of flour...weaver of cloth . . . vast producer of the comforts of life. This is *your* America.

...Keep it Free!

This is America..

...where you can listen to your radio in your living room – – not in a hideout. Where you are free to hear both sides of a question and form your own opinion ★ *This is your America*

...Keep it Free!

This is America..

. . . Not only huge cities towering to the skies . . . but, rather, the free enterprise and the free labor that built them — creating a new civilization upon the cornerstone of freedom ★ *This is your America*

...Keep it Free!

This is America..

"Smile--man--smile. You're an American... free to speak . . . free to worship . . . free to work . . . free to live in your own way. Stay on the job. This is *your* America."

...Keep it Free!

"Every rivet we drive — every bolt we turn — every ounce we sweat, brings victory a little closer. Breaking production records is the American way of doing things!"

PRODUCE FOR VICTORY!

"Keep 'em rolling, pal. On the production line, we're fighters, too. We'll give 'em a beating they'll never forget."

PRODUCE FOR VICTORY!

"Guts...and sweat...that's the stuff victory is made of! We're fighting this war to WIN... and every mother's son of us is doing his job .... Who said, *America is soft?*"

PRODUCE FOR VICTORY!

ALL: 1942. THE SHELDON-CLAIRE COMPANY

"Man for man, America's workers and America's soldiers are the best in the world! We helped them build our nation ... we'll help them defend it."

PRODUCE FOR VICTORY!

The images on posters were not haphazardly created. The selection of an "average Joe" to personify American workers was targeted to gain the "common man's" allegiance to production goals. The average working woman, on the other hand, was idealized as a fashion model in denim. This carefully glamorized image, specialists explained, was intended to convince women that they would not have to sacrifice their femininity or attractiveness for war work.

The posters typically presented women war workers as young, white, and often middle class. In truth, the majority of those who entered war-production factories were working-class wives, widows, and single women, who had been in the labor force before and chose manufacturing jobs because they paid higher wages. The symbolic image, nonetheless, helped to reinforce the temporary role that government and business planners wanted these new employees to play. Production managers expected women to fill vacated jobs during the conflict and go home once veterans returned. Historian Maureen Honey noted in *Creating Rosie the Riveter*: "For a variety of reasons, [female] war workers served as a symbol of the ideal home-front spirit, standing for national unity, dedication to the cause, and stoic pursuit of victory. This image both idealized women as a strong, capable fighter infused with a holy spirit and undercut the notion that women deserved and wanted a larger role in public life."[63]

The same could be said of establishing a larger role in industry for working men. Although the rhetoric of the war and the posters on the wall called for a new partnership between managers and workers, many industrial planners wished to see this too come to an end after the war. Business leaders anticipated that they would eventually reassert their decision-making authority, free from labor and government interference.[64]

I'm Proud... my husband wants me to do my part
SEE YOUR U. S. EMPLOYMENT SERVICE
WAR MANPOWER COMMISSION

1944. WAR MANPOWER COMMISSION

1942. BARRETT DIVISION, ALLIED CHEMICAL AND DYE CORPORATION

The posters also served to help reconstruct a positive image of business and American capitalism that had been badly shaken during the 1930s. The Depression had caused many to question large corporations' ability to lead in matters of economic and social policy. Through aggressive advertising campaigns, public-relations specialists turned this image around during the war. By arguing the superiority of America's industrial might over the enemy, and pointing out how eagerly companies rose to the national emergency, these campaigns began to restore the reputation of corporations. Business critics recognized the value of these public-relations campaigns. Richard Rovere pointed out:

> Executives see it this way. Right now, industry is regarded by the public as having done a good job in wartime and labor is in disfavor. If the point is continually hammered home that industry, in spite of labor, has done this stupendous job, then the postwar world will accept lower taxes and fewer restrictions on profits, along with more political cooperation from industry....There can be no doubt that the promotion of war campaigns has been a sincere and single-minded effort by some advertisers. There is as little doubt that it is, in the minds of most advertisers, not only good patriotism but excellent public relations....By a combination of brag and exclusive patriotism, the groundwork is laid for the sale of political and economic ideas.[65]

Even the National Association of Manufacturers (NAM) found this bragging excessive at times. Towards the end of the war the NAM vice-president noted: "If this trend kept up, the boys in the foxholes would, on their return, be forced to employ a press agent to convince the public that soldiers, too, had something to do with our victory."[66]

DEAR GOD, keep them safe!

BUY WAR BONDS and STAMPS

FOURTH READER

Published in the interest of the War Effort by the KROGER GROCERY & BAKING COMPANY

1942. KROGER GROCERY AND BAKING COMPANY

War imagery posed a problem for some retailers, for whom advertisements of self-sacrifice, conservation, and thrift ran counter to typical messages of spend and use-up. The window posters of the Kroger Grocery and Baking Company turned instead to fantasies of grim possibilities.

before it's TOO LATE!

BUY
WAR
BONDS
and STAMPS

PUBLISHED IN THE INTEREST OF THE WAR EFFORT BY
THE KROGER GROCERY AND BAKING COMPANY

1942. KROGER GROCERY AND BAKING COMPANY

1942. KROGER GROCERY AND BAKING COMPANY

MAKE THIS PLEDGE:

I pay no more than top legal prices

I accept no rationed goods
without giving up ration stamps

★ ━━━━━━━━━━━━━━━━━━━━━ ★

N.D. U.S. OFFICE OF ECONOMIC
STABILIZATION

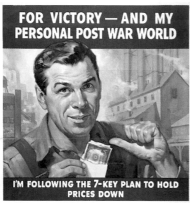

FOR VICTORY — AND MY
PERSONAL POST WAR WORLD

I'M FOLLOWING THE 7-KEY PLAN TO HOLD
PRICES DOWN

1. Buy and hold War Bonds.
2. Pay willingly our share of taxes.
3. Provide adequate life insurance and savings for our future.
4. Reduce our debts as much as possible.
5. Buy only what we need and make what we have last longer.
6. Follow ration rules and price ceilings.
7. Cooperate with our Government's wage stabilization program.

N.D. DISTRIBUTED BY THE OWI FOR THE
OFFICE OF ECONOMIC STABILIZATION

COST OF LIVING IN TWO WARS

LAST WAR →

← THIS WAR

Keep up the good work
Keep down living costs

PAY NO MORE THAN CEILING PRICES

N.D. UNATTRIBUTED

Despite war restrictions, America's living standard is still the world's best —— thanks to U.S. industrial progress.

N.D. UNATTRIBUTED

MAKE TODAY *a Safe day*

HEADQUARTERS INDUSTRIAL RELATIONS

N.D. WESTINGHOUSE HEADQUARTERS INDUSTRIAL RELATIONS

Warning against the consequences of inflation, the "Retail Activities Campaign" of the Office of Economic Stabilization encouraged women to avoid paying black-market prices for food and other items, among their responsibilities as wartime homemakers.

With the war's successful conclusion in sight, businesses turned toward idealized images of the comforts and conveniences of life, far from the factory scene of production, hoping to prepare the viewer for a world unfettered by government rationing and price controls.

By 1944, the poster had become a loaded symbol of activism and engagement on the American home front. The poster's place in expressing American war aims called forth the aesthetic values and judgments of illustrators and art directors, whose demonstrations of skill and technique took priority over the democratic aspirations of made-by-all art. Their demonstrations of expertise, like advertising, were more notable for their seen-by-all distribution. With the winding-down of the war, the poster returned to the familiar frame of political campaigns, bulletin boards, and paid space.

Dwarfed by the commercial dominance of radio and the reintroduction of the fledgling television system, the poster nonetheless played a smaller role as a winning expression of business's confidence in the future.

1944. UNATTRIBUTED

FACING PAGE | *Two members of the CIO political action committee making up posters supporting the reelection campaign of President Roosevelt, August 1944. The CIO displayed posters in union halls, department stores, and lobbies.*

Teamwork Is Important!

More and MORE and MORE these days,
TEAMWORK is the thing that pays,
It helps your company keep ahead
Of competition — — need more be said?

1953. BUREAU OF BUSINESS PRACTICE

CARD-PUNCHER CARL

At punching time clocks Carl is swell
He does it for the bunch,
Some day he'll find he hasn't got
A card of his own to punch!

1951. NATIONAL FOREMEN'S INSTITUTE, INC.

LISTEN TO JOB INSTRUCTIONS!

When your foreman instructs you — he's really sincere —
So do like the Romans did — LEND HIM YOUR EAR:
It pays in the long run, as you can well guess,
The WORK will be BETTER — the WASTE will be LESS!

1953. NATIONAL FOREMEN'S INSTITUTE, INC.

ACT YOUR AGE,
USE YOUR **NOODLE**
ON WALLS AND DOORS
PLEASE DON'T **DOODLE**!

1951. NATIONAL FOREMEN'S INSTITUTE, INC.

Cliches, cartoons, and humor dominated many of the work incentive posters that appeared in the postwar era. With the urgency of the war no longer a useful motivating theme, workplace posters often had a condescending air that was reminiscent of a parent lecturing an undisciplined child.

"If I went to work in a factory the first thing I'd do would be TO JOIN A UNION"

Franklin D. Roosevelt

N.D. CIO RESEARCH AND EDUCATION DEPARTMENT

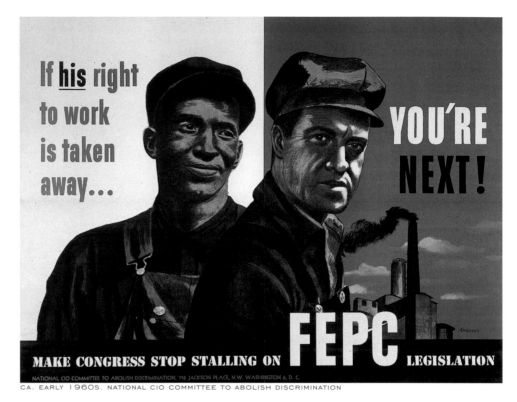

If his right to work is taken away... YOU'RE NEXT!

MAKE CONGRESS STOP STALLING ON FEPC LEGISLATION

NATIONAL CIO COMMITTEE TO ABOLISH DISCRIMINATION, 718 JACKSON PLACE, N.W. WASHINGTON 6, D. C.

CA. EARLY 1960S. NATIONAL CIO COMMITTEE TO ABOLISH DISCRIMINATION

The removal of barriers to employer speech by the Taft-Hartley Act of 1947 opened the workplace to yet a new round of anti-union discourse in the form of employee picture magazines, pamphlet racks, and posters. In response, the posters of the CIO and the AFL became a regular feature of publicity that linked union membership to the hard-won gains of the past.

Organized labor developed posters for union halls and other public places promoting social goals in the areas of civil rights, health insurance, education, and wages.

The poster's wartime service in the sale of political, social, and economic ideas provided a readily understood method for promoting postwar solidarity, rather than unanimity, among competing interest groups. Not since World War II have government, business, and labor used a wide array of posters as a major form of communication.

CA. EARLY 1960S CIO DEPARTMENT OF RESEARCH AND EDUCATION

CA. EARLY 1960S. AFL-CIO

CA. 1948. CIO POLITICAL ACTION COMMITTEE

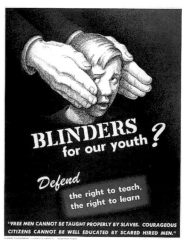

CA. EARLY 1950S. CIO DEPARTMENT
OF RESEARCH AND EDUCATION

CA. LATE 1940S. CIO DEPARTMENT OF RESEARCH AND EDUCATION

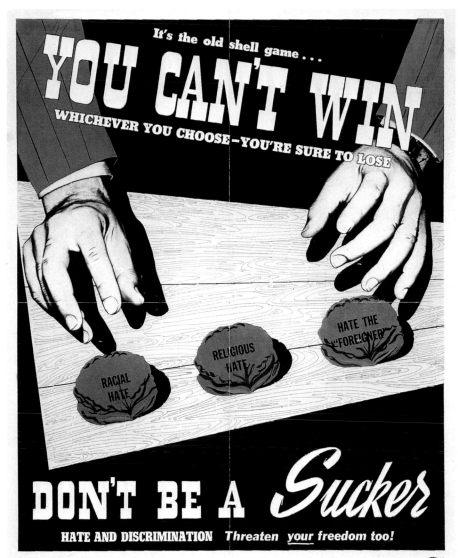

CA. EARLY 1950S. NATIONAL CIO COMMITTEE TO ABOLISH DISCRIMINATION

INTRO

1. R. P. Tolman to National Process Company, 25 August 1942, accession file 163860, National Museum of American History, Smithsonian Institution, Washington, DC.

2. Outdoor Advertising Association, Inc., *Outdoor Advertising: A Channel of Communication in the War Effort* (Chicago: Outdoor Advertising Association, ca. 1944).

CHAPTER ONE

3. Alfred M. Frankenfurter, "The Place of the Poster," *Art News* 42 (August–September, 1942): 9, 44–45.

4. Walter F. Conway to Glen L. Alt, 9 November 1942, folder: OWI Misc., box 1138, E-243, NC-148, Records of the Office of War Information, RG 208, National Archives at College Park, MD (hereafter NACP).

5. Thomas D. Mabry, "Outline for the Coordination of Government War Graphics," 1 June 1942, folder: Division of Visual Arts, box 55, E-7, RG 208, NACP.

6. OWI's poster distribution system was designed by Fred Werts, the president of the Window Display Advertising Company, who had been in charge of government poster distribution in the First World War, and Thomas Luckenbill of J. Walter Thompson, a manager of philanthropic campaigns for, among others, the Navy Relief Society. See Mabry, "Outline for the Coordination of Government War Graphics."

7. U.S. Office of War Information, *Poster Handbook. A Plan for Displaying Official War Posters* (Washington, DC: Government Printing Office, ca. 1943).

8. "Posters for Factories," *Time* 37 (7 March 1941): 23; "Bulletin Board Patriotism," *Time* 38 (28 July 1941): 57.

9. U.S. War Production Board, *Poster Catalog* (Washington, DC: G.P.O., 1942); "Best Use of Posters," *Business Week* (31 October 1942): 32.

10. U.S. War Production Board, "War Production Drive," Progress Report No. 2, 1942, folder: production drive, box 1379, entry 257, NC-148, RG 208, NACP.

CHAPTER TWO

11. Duncan Phillips, "The Arts in Wartime," *Art News* 41 (August–September, 1942): 20, 45ff.

12. Mimeograph, U.S. Office of War Information Graphics Division, *How to Make and Reproduce Posters* (New York: U.S. Office of War Information Graphics Division, ca. 1943). Contributors included Thomas M. Folds, Art Director, the Phillips Exeter Academy; Harry Sternberg and Will Barnet, Art Students League; and Anthony Velonis, Technical Director of the Creative Printmakers Group. On the influence of WPA's mimeographed handbooks see Francis V. O'Conner, ed., *The New Deal Art Projects: An Anthology of Memoirs* (Washington, DC: Smithsonian Institution Press, 1972), 168, 324.

13. Christopher DeNoon, *Posters of the WPA* (Los Angeles: Wheatley Press in association with the University of Washington Press, 1987), 17, 31–32; Richard D. McKinzie, *The New Deal for Artists* (Princeton, NJ: Princeton University Press, 1972), 168–69.

14. Typescript, Jarvis M. Morse, "Paying for a World War: The United States Financing of World War II" (Washington, DC: United States Treasury Department Library, ca. 1971), 16, 40–45; John Morton Blum, *V Was for Victory: Politics and American Culture During World War II* (New York: Harcourt, Brace, Jovanovich, 1976), 16–21; and Lawrence R. Samuel, *Pledging Allegiance: American Identity and the Bond Drive of World War II* (Washington, DC: Smithsonian Institution Press, 1997), 14–19, 50–53ff.

15. Katharine Scarborough, "Posters Aimed At Purses," *Baltimore Sun*, 4 January 1942, sec. 1, p. 2.

16. In regard to the composition of the panel of judges, a MoMA bulletin explained, "At the request of the Army and Treasury authorities the judging was done by members of the Museum staff in consultation with two executives of the well-known advertising company, J. Walter Thompson, and representatives of government departments concerned." "Posters for Defense," *Bulletin of the Museum of Modern Art* 8 (September 1941).

17. Rosamund Frost, "It Pays to Advertise," *Art News* 42 (August–September 1943): 11–26, 38–39.

18. "Posters for Defense"; Stephen Lee Renwick, "Observations on a Poster Competition," *American Artist* (October 1941): 22–24, 38ff. A second MoMA poster competition announced in August 1942 de-emphasized the free hand of the artist in discovering a model of poster effect. Competition organizers proposed to "raise the entire standard and effectiveness of poster design, particularly through the development of a direct and powerful technique for war posters." The competition's organizers supplied artists with categories and various "choice" and "required" slogans, some endowed by corporate sponsors. The largest sponsor, R. Hoe and Company of New York, a manufacturer of rotary printing presses, donated prizes for the themes of "Production," "War Bonds," "The Nature of the Enemy," and "Loose Talk." Individual sponsors included industrialist Sam A. Lewisohn ("Sacrifice"); Ellsworth Bunker, President of the National Sugar Refining Company ("The People Are on the March"); theatrical producer Dwight Wiman ("Slave World or Free"); and Thomas J. Watson of IBM ("Sacrifice: The Privilege of Free Men"). Competition judges included Frances Brennan, chief of the newly organized Office of War Information Graphics Division and formerly Art Director of *Fortune*; Charles T. Coiner, Art Director of A.W. Ayer & Son and consultant to OEM; artist Stuart Davis; and Monroe Wheeler, Director of Exhibitions and Publications for the Museum of Modern Art. Press release, 14 August 1942; and press release, n. d. Museum of Modern Art, New York. The winning posters appeared in *Life* 13 (21 December 1942): 54–57.

19. George A. Barnes to Archibald MacLeish, 29 December 1941, folder: posters, box 42, E-7, RG 208, OWI-OFF 1941–42 alpha subject file, NACP.

20. George A. Barnes to Morse Salisbury, 16 February 1942, folder: posters, box 42, E-7, RG 208, OWI-OFF 1941–42, alpha subject file, NACP.

21. George A. Barnes to Archibald MacLeish, 20 December 1941, folder:

posters, RG 208, box 42, E-7, OWI-OFF 1941–42, alpha subject file, NACP.

22. Doris Brian, "Record of the Poster Up to Date," *Art News* 42 (August–September, 1942): 10–12, 40–43.

23. Manny Farber, "War Posters," *New Republic* 106 (16 March 1942): 366–67.

CHAPTER THREE

24. Robert Griffith, "The Selling of America: The Advertising Council and American Politics, 1942–1960," *Business History Review* 57 (Autumn 1983): 388–412; Frank Fox, *Madison Avenue Goes to War: The Strange Military Career of American Advertising, 1941–1945* (Provo, UT: Brigham Young University Press, 1975), 49–51; Harold B. Thomas, "The Background and Beginning of the Advertising Council," in C. H. Sandage, *The Promise of Advertising* (Homewood, IL: Richard D. Irwin, 1961), 15–58.

25. Young & Rubicam conducted the poster survey in Toronto, March 16–April 1, 1942. "How to Make Posters that Will Help Win the War," box 12, item C, William B. Lewis papers, Boston University Library.

26. "Facts & Figures: Real Results of Polls & Surveys," *Art News* 42 (August–September 1942): 14–15, 43.

27. Ibid.; "War Posters," *Time* 40 (31 August 1942): 54.

28. William Bell and William B. Lewis to Archibald MacLeish, 3 February 1942, folder: general memoranda, box 5, OEM-OFF, Henry F. Pringle papers, Manuscript division, Library of Congress (hereafter LC).

29. Ibid.

30. "First Government Statement on Artists' Part in the War," *Art News* 42 (August–September, 1942): insert.

31. "A Portfolio of Posters," *Fortune* 24 (August 1941): 79–93.

32. Alan Cranston to Norman Ferguson, 17 November 1942, folder: California trip, box 1078, entry E222, NC 148, RG 208, NACP.

33. Penelope A. Hummel, "Fighting the War on Two Fronts: Robert Deiz and the Tuskegee Airmen," *Oregon Heritage* (Fall 1994): 40–42.

34. Norman Rockwell, *Norman Rockwell: My Adventures as an Illustrator* (Garden City, NY: Doubleday, 1960), 338–43, cited in Robert B. Westbrook, "Fighting for the American Family," in *The Power of Culture: Critical Essays in American History*, edited by Richard Wightman Fox and T. J. Jackson Lears (Chicago: University of Chicago Press, 1993), 202–03. The story of the paintings and the Treasury bond tour is amply illustrated in Stuart Murray and James McCabe, *Norman Rockwell's Four Freedoms: Images That Inspire a Nation* (Stockbridge, MA: Berkshire House, 1993).

35. Fox, *Madison Avenue Goes to War*, 10, 16, 26–32, 39–41, 49–51, 92–93; Griffith, "The Selling of America"; Blum, *V Was for Victory*, 20–21; Allan M. Winkler, *The Politics of Propaganda: The Office of War Information, 1942–1945* (New Haven: Yale University Press, 1978), 62–63, 65–68, 70–71.

36. Muriel Rukeyser, "Words and Images," *New Republic* 109 (2 August 1943): 140–42; Sydney Weinberg, "What to Tell America: The Writers' Quarrel in the Office of War Information," *Journal of American History* 55 (June 1968): 73–89; Blum, *V Was for Victory*, 38–39; Winkler, *The Politics of Propaganda*, 62–65.

37. Frances Brennan to Elmer Davis, 6 April 1943, general corresp., folder: D 1941–43, box 1, Pringle papers, LC, cited in Fox, *Madison Avenue Goes to War*, 52.

38. Typescript, rough draft of article by Jacques DunLany, Chief Bureau of Graphics, 20 September 1944, folder: Art Directors Annual Article, box 1151, E-250, NC-148, RG 208, NACP.

39. DunLany typescript, attached to letter, James D. Herbert to Chester Bowles, 1 August 1945, folder: Chester Bowles article, box 1150, E-250, NC-148, RG 208, NACP; James Brackett to Gertrude E. Schwarz, February 8, 1945, folder: OWI misc., box 1138, E-243, NC-148, RG 208, NACP.

40. "The Poster *Works* in the War," folder: poster show at S.I. June 17th, box 1151, E-250, NC-148, RG 208, NACP.

41. "Posters Based on Pacific War," n.d., and Jim Herbert to Volunteer Art Directors Committee, 5 September 1944, folder: 6th War Loan Sketches Art Directors, box 1151, E-250, NC-148, RG 208, NACP.

42. Gordon C. Aymar to James Herbert, 1 September 1944, folder: 6th War Loan Sketches Art Directors, box 1151, E-250, NC-148, RG 208, NACP.

43. Herbert to Volunteer Art Directors Committee, 4 September 1944, folder: 6th War Loan Sketches Art Directors, box 1151, E-250, NC-148, RG 208, NACP. In contrast to the Treasury's stated copy policy, George H. Roeder, Jr. notes that near the end of the war other government posters used photographs of casualties that officials considered to be "the most powerful weapons in their motivational arsenal." Roeder, *The Censored War: American Visual Experience During World War Two* (New Haven: Yale University Press, 1993), 25.

44. "Copy Policy for 7th War Loan," n.d., folder: 7th War Loan—ADS, box 1151, E-250, NC-148, RG 208, NACP.

45. Harford Powel, "What the War Has Done to Advertising," *Public Opinion Quarterly* 6 (Summer 1942): 195–203; Robert Bendiner, "Vox Populi, Inc." *Nation* 156 (17 March 1943): 449–50; Madison Avenue, "Advertising in Wartime," *New Republic* 110 (21 February 1944): 233–36.

CHAPTER FOUR

46. *Historical Statistics of the United States, Colonial Times to 1970, Bicentennial Edition, Part 1* (Washington, DC: United States Bureau of the Census, 1975), 178–79.

47. Melvyn Dubofsky, *The State and Labor in Modern America* (Chapel Hill: University of North Carolina Press, 1994), 172–73.

48. *Historical Statistics of the United States*, 178–79.

49. Dubofsky, *The State and Labor*, 172.

50. War Victory Committee, "Statement of Policy of Labor's Victory Board," issued by the Congress of Industrial Organizations and the American Federation of Labor, Office of Secretary-Treasurer, George Meany, American Federation of Labor, folder 4, War Victory Committee 1942, box 3, collection 7, George Meany Memorial Archives, Silver Spring, MD.

51. Presentation to Du Mont by Campbell-Ewald Company, 29 August 1950, box 46, Sales and Advertising, 1950, Allen B. Du Mont Laboratories papers, LC.

52. Allegheny Steel Corporation, *Steel Horizons* (1942). 2.

53. S. D. Warren Company, *Posters Used by American Industries as War Production Incentives* (Boston: S. D. Warren Company, 1942), 1, Political History Collections, National Museum of American History, Smithsonian Institution.

54. The term "production soldier" was widely used on government and privately issued posters. Cyrus Hungerford has been credited as the first poster designer to use the phrase on a series of poster in 1941. See Derek Nelson, *The Posters that Won the War: The Production, Recruitment and War Bond Posters of WWII* (Osceola, WI: Motorbooks, 1991), 62.

55. Sanford M. Jacoby, "Union-Management Cooperation in the United States during the Second World War," in *Technological Change and Workers' Movements*, edited by Melvyn Dubofsky (Beverly Hills, CA: Sage Publications, 1985), 108–9.

56. "Basic Steps Outlined for Forming an L-M Committee," October 1943, Office of the President, William Green, American Federation of Labor, folder 9, War Production Board Subject Files, 1942–1946, box 3, collection 4, George Meany Memorial Archives.

57. Jacoby, "Union-Management Cooperation in the United States," 112; Joel Seidman, *American Labor from Defense to Reconversion* (Chicago: University of Chicago Press, 1953), 176–79.

58. Leaflet, T. K. Quinn, Director, General War Production Drive, "We Need More L-M Committees," October 1943, Office of the President, William Green, American Federation of Labor, folder 9, War Production Board Subject Files, 1942–1946, box 3, collection 4, George Meany Memorial Archives.

59. Nelson Lichtenstein, *Labor's War at Home: The CIO in World War II* (Cambridge: Cambridge University Press, 1982), 90.

60. Jacoby, "Union-Management Cooperation in the United States," 115, 120.

61. *Historical Statistics of the United States,* 178–79.

CHAPTER FIVE

62. Sheldon-Claire Co, *Employee Understanding: A Monthly Newsletter Devoted to Employee Motivation*, (27 January 1959): 1–6.

63. Maureen Honey, *Creating Rosie the Riveter: Class, Gender, and Propaganda during World War II* (Amherst, MA: University of Massachusetts Press, 1984), 6, 20–24.

64. During the war, this idea of a permanent new labor-management relationship become popular among workers. In 1943, *Fortune* magazine reported "that workers not only want a fair share in the profits of the war boom but also a share in the responsibilities of management." According to their survey 74.8% factory workers believed a labor representative should be on Board of Directors, and most workers surveyed thought they should have a voice in working conditions, wages, promotions, and production plans. "The Fortune Survey," *Fortune* 27 (February, 1943): 9.

65. Richard H. Rovere, "Advertising in Wartime," *New Republic* (21 February 1944): 234–35.

66. Ibid.

BIBLIOGRAPHY

BOOKS

Ades, Dawn, et al. *The 20th Century Poster: Design of the Avant-Garde*. New York: Abbeville Press, 1984.

Alexandre, Arsene, et al. *The Modern Poster*. New York: Charles Scribner's Sons, 1895.

Art and Psychological Warfare: World War II Posters. Hempstead, NY: Emily Lowe Gallery, Hofstra University, 1982.

Art Directors Club of New York. *24th Art Directors Annual*. New York: Art Directors Club, 1942.

Anderson, Karen. *Wartime Women: Sex Roles, Family Relations, and the Status of Women During World War II*. Westport, CT: Greenwood Press, 1981.

Association of National Advertisers. *The Job Ahead for Business: Selling the Company Behind the Product*. New York: Association of National Advertisers, 1946.

Barnicoat, John. *A Concise History of Posters: 1870–1970*. New York: Harry N. Abrams, 1972.

Blum, John Morton. *V Was for Victory: Politics and American Culture During World War II*. New York: Harcourt, Brace, Jovanovich, 1976.

Bolton, Charles Knowles. *The Reign of the Poster, Being Comments and Criticisms*. Boston: W. B. Jones, 1895.

Casdorph, Paul D. *"Let the Good Times Roll": Life at Home in America During World War II*. New York: Paragon House, 1989.

Cochrane, Ira Lee. *Display Animation 1939–40. The Yearbook of Motion Displays*. New York: Reede & Morton, 1940.

Crawford, Anthony R., ed. *Posters of World War I and World War II in the George C. Marshall Research Foundation*. Charlottesville: University of Virginia Press, 1979.

Crowell, Benedict, and Robert Forrest Wilson. *The Armies of Industry*. New Haven: Yale University Press, 1921.

———. *The Giant Hand: Our Mobilization and Control of Industry and Natural Resources, 1917–1918*. New Haven: Yale University Press, 1921.

Daniel, Pete, et al. *Official Images: New Deal Photography*. Washington, DC: Smithsonian Institution Press, 1987.

Darracourt, Joseph, and Belinda Loftus. *Second World War Posters*, 2d ed. London: Imperial War Museum, 1981.

DeNoon, Christopher. *Posters of the WPA*. Los Angeles: Wheatley Press in association with the University of Washington Press, 1987.

Doss, Erika Lee. *Benton, Pollock, and the Politics of Modernism: From Regionalism to Abstract Expressionism*. Chicago: University of Chicago Press, 1991.

Dreisziger, N. F. ed. *Mobilization for Total War: The Canadian, American, and British Experience, 1914–1918, 1939–1945*. Waterloo, Canada: Wilfrid Laurier University Press, 1981.

Ellul, Jacques. *Propaganda: The Formation of Men's Attitudes*. New York: Knopf, 1965.

Fox, Frank W. *Madison Avenue Goes to War: The Strange Military Career of American Advertising, 1941–1945*. Provo, UT: Brigham Young University Press, 1975.

Fox, Richard Wightman and T. J. Jackson Lears, eds. *The Power of Culture: Critical Essays in American History.* Chicago: University of Chicago Press, 1993.

Franklin Institute. *New Poster International Exposition of Design in Outdoor Advertising.* Philadelphia: Franklin Institute, 1937.

Gaer, Joseph. *The First Round: The Story of the CIO Political Action Committee.* New York: Duell, Sloan and Pearce, 1944.

General Cable Corporation. *Fight Talk.* New York: General Cable Corporation, 1945.

General Electric Company. *More Goods for More People at Less Cost. A Tribute to American Industry.* New York: General Electric Co., 1940.

General Motors Corporation. *American Battle for Abundance: A Story of Mass Production.* Detroit: General Motors, 1947.

———. *My Job and Why I Like It.* Detroit: General Motors, 1947.

Grolier Club, New York. *Catalogue of and Exhibition of Illustrated Bill-Posters.* New York: The De Vinne Press, 1890.

Hall, Edward Hagaman. *The Poster Nuisance. An Argument Against the Abuse of Outdoor Advertising.* Albany, NY, 1905.

Halley, William C. *Employee Publications: Theory and Practice of Communications in the Modern Organization.* Philadelphia: Chilton Co. Book Division, 1959.

Harper, Paula. *War, Revolution and Peace. Propaganda Posters from the Hoover Institution Archives, 1941–1945.* Stanford, CA, ca. 1972.

Harrington, Burton. *The Essentials of Poster Design.* Chicago: Poster Advertising Association, Inc., 1925.

Harris, Howell John. *The Right to Manage: Industrial Relations Policies of American Business in the 1940s.* Madison: University of Wisconsin Press, 1982.

Hartmann, Susan M. *The Home Front and Beyond: American Women in the 1940s.* Boston: Twayne Publishers, 1982.

Hawkins, George Henry Edward. *Poster Advertising: Being A Talk on the Subject of Posting as an Advertising Medium.* Chicago, 1910.

Honey, Maureen. *Creating Rosie the Riveter: Class, Gender, and Propaganda During World War II.* Amherst: University of Massachusetts Press, 1984.

Jenkins, Alan. *The Forties.* New York: Universe Books, 1977.

Judd, Denis. *Posters of World War Two.* New York: St. Martins's Press, 1973.

Lerner, Daniel. *Paper Bullets: Great Propaganda Posters, Axis & Allied Countries WW II.* New York: Chelsea House Publishers, 1977.

Lichtenstein, Nelson. *Labor's War at Home: The CIO in World War II.* New York: Cambridge University Press, 1982.

Lingeman, Richard R. *Don't You Know There's a War On? The American Home Front, 1941–1945.* New York: G. P. Putnam's Sons, 1970.

McCamy, James L. *Government Publicity: Its Practice in Federal Administration.* University of Chicago Press, 1939.

McKinzie, Richard D. *The New Deal for Artists.* Princeton, NJ: Princeton University Press, 1973.

Marchand, Roland. *Advertising the American Dream: Making Way for Modernity, 1920–1940.* Berkeley: University of California Press, 1985.

Marling, Karal Ann. *Norman Rockwell.* New York: Harry N. Abrams, 1997.

Massachusetts Charitable Mechanic Association. *Exhibition of Posters, October 2 to November 30, 1895.* Boston: Massachusetts Charitable Mechanic Association, 1895.

May, Lary, ed. *Recasting America: Culture and Politics in the Age of Cold War.* Chicago: University of Chicago Press, 1989.

Mercer, Frank A., ed. *Modern Publicity.* London: Studio Publications, 1941.

Meyer, Susan E. *America's Great Illustrators.* New York: Harry N. Abrams, 1978.

Molella, Arthur P. *FDR: The Intimate Presidency. Franklin D. Roosevelt, Communication, and the Mass Media in the 1930s.* Washington, DC: Smithsonian Institution, 1982.

Morrison, Ellen Earnhardt. *Guardian of the Forest: A History of the Smokey Bear Program.* New York: Vantage Press, 1976.

Moss, Michael E. *Posters for Victory: The American Homefront and World War II.* West Point: United States Military Academy, 1978.

Murray, Stuart, and James McCabe. *Norman Rockwell's Four Freedoms: Images That Inspire A Nation.* Stockbridge, MA: Berkshire House, 1993.

Museum of Modern Art. *Word and Image: Posters from the Collection of the Museum of Modern Art.* Text by Alan M. Fern. Greenwich, CT: New York Graphic Society, 1968.

———. *Posters for Defense. Exhibition held at the Museum of Modern Art, September 24–October 6, 1941.* New York: Museum of Modern Art, 1941.

National Archives and Records Administration. *Broadsides and Posters from the National Archives.* Washington: National Archives and Records Administration, 1986.

National Association of Manufacturers. *Posters for Production.* New York: National Association of Manufacturers, 1943.

National Collection of Fine Arts. *Images of An Era: The American Poster, 1945–75.* Washington, DC: National Collection of Fine Arts, Smithsonian Institution, 1975.

National Opinion Research Center. *Display of an O.W.I. Poster, "The Cost of Living"* (Study S-52), 1944.

———. *Memo: Public Estimate of War Posters' Effectiveness* (Study 121), 1943.

National Safety Council. *Directory [of] Occupational Safety Posters.* Chicago: National Safety Council, ca. 1949.

Nelson, Derek. *The Posters that Won the War.* Osceola, WI: Motorbooks International, 1991.

O'Connor, Francis V., ed. *The New Deal Art Projects. An Anthology of Memoirs.* Washington, DC: Smithsonian Institution Press, 1972.

———. *Art for the Millions: Essays from the 1930s by Artists and Administrators of the WPA Federal Art Project.* Boston: New York Graphic Society, 1975.

Outdoor Advertising Association. *Advertising Outdoors.* Chicago: Outdoor Advertising Association of America, Inc., 1930–31.

———. *Outdoor Advertising, A Channel of Communication in the War Effort.* Chicago: Outdoor Advertising Association of America, Inc., 1944.

———. *Record of War Activities of the Outdoor Advertising Industry, World War II.* Chicago: Outdoor Advertising Association of America, ca. 1948.

Pitz, Henry C. *200 Years of American Illustration.* New York: Random House, 1977.

Polenberg, Richard. *America at War: The Home Front, 1941–1945.* Englewood Cliffs, NJ: Prentice-Hall, 1968.

———. *War and Society: The United States, 1941–1945.* Philadelphia: J. B. Lippincott, 1972.

Price, Charles Matlack, and Horace Brown. *How to Put in Patriotic Posters the Stuff That Makes People Stop—Look—Act!* Washington, DC: National Committee of Patriotic Societies, 1918.

Rawls, Walton H. *Wake Up, America! World War I and the American Poster.* New York: Abbeville Press, 1988.

Reed, Walt, and Roger Reed. *The Illustrator in America, 1880–1980: A Century of Illustration.* New York: Madison Square Press, 1984.

Rhodes, Anthony Richard Ewart. *Propaganda: The Art of Persuasion in World War II.* New York: Chelsea House, 1976.

Rickards, Maurice. *The Rise and Fall of the Poster.* New York: McGraw-Hill Book Company, 1971.

Riesman, David. *Abundance for What? And Other Essays.* Garden City, NJ: Doubleday, 1964.

Rockwell, Norman. *Norman Rockwell: My Adventures as an Illustrator.* Garden City, NY: Doubleday, 1960.

Roeder, George H. Jr. *The Censored War: American Visual Experience During World War Two.* New Haven: Yale University Press, 1993.

Routzahn, Mary Brayton. *Traveling Publicity Campaigns: Educational Tours of Railroad Trains and Motor Vehicles.* New York: Russell Sage Foundation, 1920.

Rupp, Leila J. *Mobilizing Women for War: German and American Propaganda, 1939–1945.* Princeton, NJ: Princeton University Press, 1978.

Samuel, Lawrence R. *Pledging Allegiance: American Identity and the Bond Drive of World War II.* Washington, DC: Smithsonian Institution Press, 1997.

Sandage, C. H. *The Promise of Advertising.* Homewood, IL: Richard D. Irwin, 1961.

S. D. Warren Company. *Posters Used by American Industries as War Production Incentives.* Boston: S. D. Warren Company, 1942.

St. Clair, Labert. *The Story of the Liberty Loans.* Washington, DC: James William Bryan Press, 1919.

Shaw, Charles K. *Industrial Publicity.* London: C. & J. Temple Limited, 1944.

Stanley, Peter. *What Did You Do in the War, Daddy? A Visual History of Propaganda Posters.* New York: Oxford University Press, 1983.

Steele, Richard W. *Propaganda in an Open Society: The Roosevelt Administration and the Media, 1933–1941.* Westport, CT: Greenwood Press, 1985.

Stott, William. *Documentary Expression and Thirties America.* Chicago: University of Chicago Press, 1986.

Sutton, Francis X., et al. *The American Business Creed.* Cambridge, MA: Harvard University Press, 1956.

Tedlow, Richard S. *Keeping the Corporate Image: Public Relations and Business, 1900–1950.* Greenwich, CT: JAI Press, 1979.

Teitelbaum, Matthew, ed. *Montage and Modern Life, 1919–1942.* Cambridge, MA: MIT Press, 1992.

Tovell, Rosemarie, and Karl Schutt. *Posters from Three Wars.* Ottawa: National Gallery of Canada, 1969.

United States. *Industrial Mobilization for War: History of the War Production Board and Predecessor Agencies, 1940–1945,* vol 1. Washington, DC: Government Printing Office, 1947.

United States. National Gallery of Art. *American Artists' Record of War and Defense. Watercolors, Drawings, and Prints Purchased by the Office for Emergency Management from Entries Submitted to the Section of Fine Arts in an Open, National Competition.* Washington, DC: National Gallery of Art, 1942.

United States. Office of War Information. *How to Make and Reproduce Posters.* New York: Office of War Information, Bureau of Graphics and Printing, ca. 1943.

———. *Poster Handbook—A Plan for Displaying Official War Posters.* Washington, DC: Government Printing Office, 1943.

United States. Treasury Department. National Committee of Honorary Patrons. *A National Exhibition of Original Paintings by American Artists Designed for Poster Use.* Washington, DC: ca. 1943.

United States. War Production Board. *Official Plan Book of the War Production Drive.* Washington, DC: Government Printing Office, ca. 1942.

———. *Poster Catalog.* Washington, DC: Government Printing Office, ca. 1942.

———. *Production Charts.* Washington, DC: Government Printing Office, ca. 1942.

———. *War Production Drive Progress Report No. 2.* Washington, DC: Government Printing Office, ca. 1942. In folder: Production Drive, box: 1379, entry 148, RG 208, OWI, Modern Military Branch, National Archives and Records Administration, Suitland, MD.

Walker, Strother Holland, and Paul Sklar. *Business Finds Its Voice.* New York: Harper & Brothers, 1938.

Weill, Alain. *The Poster: A Worldwide Survey and History.* Boston: G. K. Hall & Co., 1985.

Whyte, William H. *Is Anybody Listening? How and Why U.S. Business Fumbles When It Talks with Human Beings.* New York: Simon and Schuster, 1952.

Winkler, Allan M. *Home Front U.S.A.: America During World War II.* Arlington Heights, IL: H. Davidson, 1986.

———. *The Politics of Propaganda: The Office of War Information, 1942–1945.* New Haven: Yale University Press, 1978.

Yanker, Gary. *Prop Art: Over 1000 Contemporary Political Posters.* New York: Darien House, 1972.

Young & Rubicam. *How to Make Posters That Will Help Win the War.* New York: Young & Rubicam, 1942.

Zeman, Z. A. B. *Selling the War: Art and Propaganda in World War II.* London: Orbis Books, 1978.

ARTICLES

"A Portfolio of Posters." *Fortune* 24 (19 August 1941): 79–93.

"Advertising in Wartime." *New Republic* 110 (21 February 1944): 233–36.

Allegheny Ludlum Steel Corporation. "Worker Morale Going Up!" *Steel Horizons* 4, no. 2 (1942): 2–5.

"Art By Uncle Sam." *New York Times Magazine* (11 May 1941): 6.

Bendiner, Robert. "Vox Populi, Inc." *Nation* 156 (27 March 1943): 449–50.

"Best Use of Posters." *Business Week* (31 October 1942): 32.

Bigelow, Burton. "Should Business Decentralize Its Counter-Propaganda?" *Public Opinion Quarterly* 1 (April 1938): 321–24.

"Biography of A Poster." *New York Times Magazine* (16 August 1942): 16–17.

Bradsher, James Gregory. "Taking America's Heritage to the People: The Freedom Train Story." *Prologue* 17 (Winter 1985): 228–45.

Brian, Doris. "Record of the Poster Up to Date." *Art News* 41 (August–September 1942): 10–12, 40–43.

"Bulletin Board Patriotism." *Time* 38 (28 July 1941): 57.

Calkins, E. E. "Psychology of the Poster." *International Studio* 45 (December 1911): 49–50.

Dembo, George M. "The Statue of Liberty in Posters: Creation of an American Icon." *P.S.: The Quarterly Journal of the Poster Society* (Winter 1985–1986): 18–21.

"England Says 'Hush.'" *Life* 8 (18 March 1940): 47–48.

Farber, Manny. "War Posters." *New Republic* 106 (16 March 1942): 366–67.

"Facts & Figures. Real Results of Polls & Surveys." *Art News* 41 (August–September 1942): 14–18, 43.

"First Government Statement on Artists' Part in the War." *Art News* 41 (August–September 1942): insert between 6–7.

Frankfurter, Alfred M. "The Place of the Poster." *Art News* 41 (August–September 1942): 8–9, 44–45.

Gitlin, Todd. "Mass Media Sociology: The Dominant Paradigm." *Theory and Society* 6 (September 1978): 203–53.

Griffith, Robert. "The Selling of America: The Advertising Council and American Politics, 1942–1960." *Business History Review* 57 (Autumn 1983): 388–412.

Hawkins, Lester G., Jr., and George S. Pettee. "O.W.I.—Organization and Problems." *Public Opinion Quarterly* 7 (Spring 1943): 15–33.

Hummel, Penelope A. "Fighting the War on Two Fronts: Robert Deiz and the Tuskegee Airmen." *Oregon Heritage* (Fall 1994): 40–42.

Jacobs, Meg. "'How About Some Meat?': The Office of Price Administration, Consumption Politics, and State Building from the Bottom Up, 1941–1946." *Journal of American History* 84 (December 1997): 910–41.

Leff, Mark H. "The Politics of Sacrifice on the American Home Front in World War II." *Journal of American History* 77 (March 1991): 1296–1318.

McCormick, C. D. "The Lesson of the Commercial Poster." *Art News* 41 (August–September 1942): 13, 40.

"A National Poster Contest for Artists." *Art News* 41 (August–September 1942): 19.

Odegard, Peter H., and Alan Barth. "Millions for Defense." *Public Opinion Quarterly* (Fall 1941):

Pearlin, Leonard I. and Morris Rosenberg. "Propaganda Techniques in Institution Advertising." *Public Opinion Quarterly* 16 (Spring 1952): 5–26.

Phillips, Duncan. "The Arts in Wartime." *Art News* 41 (August–September 1942): 20, 45ff.

"The Poster Front." *Art News* 41 (15–31 October 1942): 32.

———. *Art News* 41 (1–14 October 1942): 30.

"Posters and Slogans." *Nation* 104 (21 June 1917): 728.

"Posters for Factories." *Time* 37 (17 March 1941): 23.

"Posters for Victory." *New York Times Magazine* (29 November 1942): 20–21.

"Posters of World War II —And of World War I." *New York Times Magazine* (22 March 1942): 20–21.

"Posters to Sweep the United States." *Literary Digest* 57 (29 June 1918): 30.

Renwick, Stephen Lee. "Observations on a Poster Competition." *American Artist* (October 1941): 22–24, 38ff.

Rukeyser, Muriel. "Words and Images." *New Republic* 109 (2 August 1943): 140–142.

Scarborough, Katherine. "Posters Aimed At Purses." *Baltimore Sun*, 4 January 1942, sec. 1, p. 2.

"Shut Up, America." *Life* 12 (9 February 1942): 36–37.

"Speaking of Pictures . . ." *Life* 10 (24 March 1941): 12–13, 15.

Sullivan, Lawrence. "Government By Mimeograph." *Atlantic Monthly* 161 (March 1938): 306–15.

"'The Walls Have Ears.'" *New York Times Magazine* (4 October 1942): 11.

"The War Poster." *Nation* 107 (14 September 1918): 303–304.

"War Poster Factory." *New York Times Magazine* (5 April 1942): 23.

"War Posters." *Life* 13 (21 December 1942): 54–57.

"War Posters." *Time* 40 (31 August 1942): 54.

"War Posters Roasted." *Newsweek* 20 (17 August 1942): 72.

Weinberg, Sydney. "What to Tell America: The Writers' Quarrel in the Office of War Information." *Journal of American History* 55 (June 1968): 73–89.

UNPUBLISHED

Fehl, Philipp. "A Stylistic Analysis of Some Propaganda Posters of World War II." (M.A. thesis, Stanford University, California, 1948).

Morse, Jarvis M. "Paying for a World War: The United States Financing of World War II." Washington, DC: United States Treasury Department Library, ca. 1971.

Olney, Lawrence M. "The War Bond Story." Washington, DC: U.S. Treasury Department Library, ca. 1971.

24 BOTTOM. artist: Jean Carlu, gift of Mrs. D. R. Martin, cat. 1978.2348.26, 40 ⅛" x 30 ⅛", SI #84-8389-9

26. artist: Dean Cornwell, cat. 1984.0473.029, 18 ½" x 26", SI #91-2546

29 TOP LEFT. artist: Jean Carlu, gift of Harris, Seybold, Potter Company, cat. 163958.01, 40" x 30" SI #94-8389

29 BOTTOM LEFT. b&w photograph by Jack Delano, courtesy U.S. Office of War Information Collection, Prints and Photographs Division, Library of Congress, LC-USW3-4783-D

29 RIGHT. gift of U.S. War Department Bureau of Public Relations, cat. 163677.01, 40" x 28 ½", SI #91-10319

30 TOP LEFT. U.S. Office of War Information poster no. 8, artist: David Stone Martin, gift of U.S. Office of War Information, Bureau of Publications and Graphics, cat. 164238.02, 22" x 28", SI #88-10638

30 BOTTOM LEFT. U.S. Office of War Information poster no. 26, artist: Bernard Perlin and David Stone Martin, cat. 1984.0473.076, 20" x 28", SI #97-8791

30 RIGHT. b&w photograph, photographer unknown, courtesy U.S. Office of War Information Collection, Prints and Photographs Division, Library of Congress, LC-USW-33-969-20

32 LEFT. U.S. Office of War Information poster no. 76, cat. 1984.0473.062, 20" x 28", SI #97-8617

32 MIDDLE. cat. 1984.0473.049, 17 ⅛" x 21 1/16", SI #97-8589

32 TOP RIGHT. artist: E. Means, cat. 1984.0473.093, 28 ¼" x 43 ¼", SI # 97-8515

32 BOTTOM RIGHT. U.S. Office of War Information poster no. 64, artist: Koerner, cat. 1984.0473.080, 28 ½" x 40", SI #97-8667

33 TOP LEFT. gift of U.S. Navy Department, Incentive Division, cat. 164870.03, 30" x 40 1/2", SI #97-8653

33 BOTTOM LEFT. U.S. Office of War Information poster no. 62, cat. 1984.0473.060, 20" x 28", SI #97-8619

33 RIGHT. artist: Jon Whitcomb, gift of U.S. Navy Department, Incentive Division, cat. 164870.04, 30" x 40", SI #97-8652

34 LEFT. U.S. Office of War Information poster no. 58, cat. 1984.0473.051, 16 3/16" x 22 ¾", SI #97-8573

34 RIGHT. artist: Weimar Pursell, cat. 1984.0473.045, 22" x 28", SI #91-2547

35 LEFT. U.S. Office of War Information poster no. 39, gift of Leon A. Whitney, cat. 1985.0776.06, 22" x 28" SI #97-8611

35 TOP RIGHT. cat. 1984.0473.089, 29" x 40 ⅛", SI #97-8651

35 BOTTOM RIGHT. U.S. Office of War Information, poster no. 74, cat. 1984.0473.015, 20" x 28", SI #97-8610

36 LEFT. gift of Leon A. Whitney, cat. 1985.0776.04, 20" x 28", SI #91-16230

36 RIGHT. U.S. Office of War Information poster no. 50, cat. 1984.0473.010, 20 ¼" x 28 ¼", SI #97-8616

37 TOP LEFT. U.S. Office of War Information poster no. 44, artist: Norman Rockwell painting for the Saturday Evening Post, gift of U.S. Office of War Information, Division of Public Inquiries, cat. 165236.05, 40 ⅛" x 56 ⅛", SI #97-8519

37 TOP MIDDLE. U.S. Office of War Information poster no. 43, artist: Norman Rockwell painting for the Saturday Evening Post, gift of U.S. Office of War Information, Division of Public Inquiries, cat. 165236.02, 40 ⅛" x 56 ⅛", SI #97-8520

37 TOP RIGHT. U.S. Office of War Information poster no. 45, artist: Norman Rockwell painting for the Saturday Evening Post, gift of U.S. Office of War Information, Division of Public Inquiries, cat. 165236.03, 40 ⅛" x 56 ⅛", SI #97-8518

37 BOTTOM. U.S. Office of War Information poster no. 46, artist: Norman Rockwell painting for the Saturday Evening Post, gift of U.S. Office of War Information, Division of Public Inquiries, cat. 165236.04, 40 ⅛" x 56 ⅛", SI #97-8516

38. U.S. Office of War Information poster no. 41, artist: Criss, cat. 1984.0473.039, 21" x 28", SI #91-2548

39. U.S. Office of War Information poster no. 57, artist: Al Parker, cat. 1984.0473.042, 16" x 22 ½", SI #87-8757

40. artist: Jon Whitcomb, cat. 1984.0473.036, 22" x 28", SI #97-8782

41 LEFT. gift of U.S. Navy Department, Incentive Division, cat. 164870.02, 30 ⅛" x 40 ¼", SI #97-8521

41 MIDDLE. U.S. Office of War Information Poster no. 78, artist: Leon Helguera, cat. 1984.0473.013, 20" x 28", SI #97-8785

41 RIGHT. artist: Jes Wilhelm Schlaikjer, cat. 1984.0473.031, 20" x 28", SI #97-8784

42. artist: Wesley Heyman, cat. 1984.0473.053, 20 ⅛" x 28", SI #97-8789

43 LEFT. artist: Montgomery Melbourne, cat. 1984.0473.058, 22" x 28", SI #97-8783

43 RIGHT. artist: Jerome Rozen, cat. 1984.0473.025, 20" x 27", SI #97-8788

44 LEFT. artist: Bernard Perlin, cat. 1984.0473.100, 28 ½" x 48 ½", SI # 97-8666

45 LEFT. artist: unknown, cat. 1984.0473.072, 22 ⅛" x 28 ⅛", SI #97-8615

45 TOP RIGHT. artist: Herbert Morton Stoops, cat. 1984.0473.075, 20" x 28", SI #97-8786

45 BOTTOM RIGHT. U.S. Office of War Information poster no. 36, artist: Anton Otto Fischer, gift of U.S. Office of War Information, Division of Public Inquiries, cat. 164824.10, 22 ⅛" x 28", SI #97-8614

46. artist: R. Moore, cat. 1984.0473.084, 41" x 29", SI #97-8779

47 LEFT. cat. 1984.0473.106, 20 ⅛" x 28", SI #97-8620

47 MIDDLE. artist: Bingham, cat. 1984.0473.016, 20 ⅛" x 27 ⅞", SI #97-8790

47 RIGHT. artist: Roy Martin, cat. 1984.0473.090, 28" x 40", SI #97-8665

48 LEFT. cat. 1984.0473.30, 20" x 28", SI #97-8990

48 RIGHT. artist: Ruth Nichols, cat. 1984.0473.054, 20 ⅛" x 28", SI #97-8984

49 LEFT. artist: Adolph Treidler, cat. 1984.0473.019, 18 ½" x 26", SI #97-8788

49 TOP RIGHT. artist: C. C. Beall, cat. 1984.0473.017, 18 ½" x 26", SI # 91-2545

49 BOTTOM RIGHT. artist: C. C. Beall, cat. 1984.0473.041, 18 ½" x 26 ⅛", SI #97-8618

50. b&w photograph by Jack Delano, courtesy U.S. Office of War Information Collection, Print and Photographs Division, Library of Congress, LC USW3-5616-D

52. artist: Ralph Iligan, gift of United Aircraft Corporation, cat. 164005.12, 16" x 20", SI # 91-16234

53 TOP LEFT. artist: Ralph Iligan, gift of United Aircraft Corporation, cat. 164005.16, 16" x 20" SI #91-16235

53 TOP RIGHT. artist: Ralph Iligan, gift of United Aircraft Corporation, cat. 164005.14, 16" x 20", SI #91-16233

53 BOTTOM LEFT. artist: Ralph Iligan, gift of United Aircraft Corporation, cat. 164005.13, 16" x 20", SI #91-16236

53 BOTTOM RIGHT. artist: Ralph Iligan, gift of United Aircraft Corporation, cat. 164005.15, 16" x 20", SI #87-11432

54. b&w photograph, 1941. Courtesy of The George Meany Memorial Archives, negative no. 392

55. artist: Pokras, cat. 1994.0102.08, 15 ¼" x 22 ¼", SI #94-9065

56. artist: Pokras, cat. 1994.0102.03, 22" x 32 1/8", SI# 94-9063

57 LEFT. artist: Whitman, gift of the American Red Cross, cat. 1978.0880.14, 22" x 31 ⅞", SI #97-8612

57 RIGHT. artist: unknown, gift of the American Red Cross, cat. 1978.0880.49, 16 ⅛ x 22", SI #97-8575

58. gift of Oldsmobile Division, General Motors Corporation, cat. 164371.43, 30" x 40", SI # 91-10322

59 TOP LEFT. gift of Oldsmobile Division, General Motors Corporation, cat. 164371.01, 30" x 40", SI # 97-8684

59 BOTTOM LEFT. gift of Oldsmobile Division, General Motors Corporation, cat. 164371.29, 30" x 40", SI # 97-8637

59 TOP MIDDLE. gift of Oldsmobile Division, General Motors Corporation, cat. 164371.05, 30" x 40", SI # 97-8680

59 BOTTOM MIDDLE. gift of Oldsmobile Division, General Motors Corporation, cat. 164371.25, 30" x 40", SI # 91-10321

59 TOP RIGHT. gift of Oldsmobile Division, General Motors Corporation, cat. 164371.37, 30" x 40", SI # 97-8647

59 BOTTOM RIGHT. gift of Oldsmobile Division, General Motors Corporation, cat. 164371.02, 30" x 40", # 97-8683

60 LEFT. gift of RCA Manufacturing Company, cat. 164349.07. 17" x 22 ⅛", SI #97-8579

60 RIGHT. gift of RCA Manufacturing Company, cat. 164349.03, 18" x 22 ⅛" SI #97-8580

61 LEFT. gift of RCA Manufacturing Company, cat. 164349.02, 18" x 22 ⅛" SI #97-8576

61 TOP RIGHT. gift of RCA Manufacturing Company, cat. 164349.04, 18" x 22 ⅛", SI #97-8578

61 MIDDLE RIGHT. gift of RCA Manufacturing Company, cat. 164349.13, 18" x 22 ⅛ , SI #97-8577

61 BOTTOM RIGHT. gift of RCA Manufacturing Company, cat. 164349.05, 18" x 22 1/8", SI #91-16238

62. gift of General Cable Corporation, cat. 164976.01, 30" x 39", SI# 91-14111

63 LEFT. artist: Norman Lewis, cat. 1994.0102.05, 19" x 28 ⅞", SI# 94-9061

63 RIGHT. gift of U.S. War Department Services of Supply, cat. 163676.06, 28" x 40", SI #91-14108

64. b&w photograph by Ann Rosener, courtesy of U.S. Office of War Information Collection, National Archives and Records Administration, NARA #RG 47-G-6W-36BX

65 LEFT. artist: Herbert Roese, gift of Nathaniel C. Spear Jr., cat. 1987.0282.115, 28" x 40", SI #97-8662

65 MIDDLE. artist: Robert Riggs, gift of Nathaniel C. Spear Jr., cat. 1987.0282.116, 28" x 40", SI #97-8663

65 RIGHT. artist: Fred Ludekens, gift of Nathaniel C. Spear Jr., cat. 1987.0282.114, 28" x 40", SI #97-8661

66. gift of Harris, Seybold, Potter Company, cat. 163958.02, 40" x 30", SI#97-8658

67 LEFT. gift of Fisher Body Division, General Motors Corporation, cat. 164393.03, 41" x 31", SI #90-460

67 RIGHT. gift of Fisher Body Division, General Motors Corporation, cat. 164393.07, 41" x 31", SI #91-10320

68. b&w photograph by Russell Aikens, History of Technology Reference Collection, National Museum of American History, Smithsonian Institution, SI #94-4377

69 LEFT. gift of Peabody Museum of Archaeology and Ethnology, cat. 303735.20, 38" x 28", SI#31-14113

69 TOP RIGHT. gift of Peabody Museum of Archaeology and Ethnology, cat. 303735.23, 28" x 38", SI#97-8657

69 BOTTOM RIGHT. artist: Harvey Ragsdale, gift of Harris, Seybold, Potter Company, cat. 163958.11, 17" x 22", SI #97-8582

70 LEFT. gift of Walter Kidde & Company, Inc., cat. 164560.13, 17" x 23", SI #91-16240

70 RIGHT. gift of Walter Kidde & Company, Inc., cat. 164560.11, 17" x 23", SI #91-16239

71 LEFT. gift of Walter Kidde & Company, Inc., cat. 164560.07, 17 ⅛" x 21 ⅞", SI #97-8558

71 RIGHT. gift of Walter Kidde & Company. Inc., cat. 164560.10, 17 ⅛" x 22", SI #97-8583

72 LEFT. cat. 1984.0473.050, 17 ⅛" x 21 ⅛", SI #97-8585

72 RIGHT. gift of S. D. Warren Company, cat. 163991.09, 40" x 28", SI #93-2312

73 TOP LEFT. gift of Peabody Museum of Archaeology and Ethnology, cat. 303735.24, 28" x 38", SI #97-8664

73 TOP RIGHT. artist: Reynold Brown, gift of North American Aviation, Inc., cat. 164814.02, 32 ½" x 42 ½", SI #91-14114

73 BOTTOM LEFT. gift of National Process Company, cat. 163800.01, 12 ⅛" x 19 ⅛", SI #97-8671

73 BOTTOM RIGHT. gift of U.S. Navy Department, Incentive Division, cat. 164870.01, 30" x 40 ⅛", SI #97-8642

74 LEFT. gift of Rogers, Kellogg, Stillson, Inc., cat. 164135.05, 15 ⅛" x 22 ⅛", SI #97-8669

74 MIDDLE. gift of Rogers, Kellogg, Stillson, Inc., cat. 164135.08, 15 ⅛" x 22 ⅛", SI #97-8586

74 RIGHT. gift of Rogers, Kellogg, Stillson, Inc., cat. 164135.07, 15 ⅛" x 22 ⅛", #97-8668

75 LEFT. artist: unknown, gift of The Employers Group, cat. 164392.08, 9" x 12", SI #88-10633

75 RIGHT. artist: Howard Scott, gift of U.S. Navy Department, Incentive Division, cat. 164870.05, 30" x 40", SI #88-106390

76 LEFT. gift of Briggs Manufacturing Company, cat. 164587.09, 28" x 42", SI #97-8656

76 RIGHT. gift of Briggs Manufacturing Company, cat. 164587.21, 28" x 42" SI #97-8654

77 LEFT. gift of Briggs Manufacturing Company, cat. 164587.14, 28" x 42", SI #97-8659

77 TOP RIGHT. gift of Briggs Manufacturing Company, cat. 164587.24, 28" x 42", SI #97-8660

77 BOTTOM RIGHT. gift of Briggs Manufacturing Company, cat. 164587.08, 28" x 42", SI #97-8655

78. artist: J. Howard Miller, gift of J. Howard Miller, cat. 1985.0851.05, 17" x 22", SI #87-13107

79. artist: J. Howard Miller, gift of J. Howard Miller, cat. 1985.0851.37, 17" x 22", SI #91-2543

80 LEFT. artist: J. Howard Miller, gift of J. Howard Miller, cat. 1985.0851.39, 17" x 22", SI #97-8542

Unless otherwise noted, all photographs are courtesy of the National Museum of American History, Smithsonian Institution.